WREN'S E

Adventures of a Visual Signaller

Stephanie Batstone

Line illustrations by the author

PARAPRESS

Also published by Parapress:

Thirty-Odd Feet Below Belgium,
an Affair of Letters in the Great War 1915-16, ed. Arthur Stockwin
Sea Soldier, an Officer of Marines with Duncan, Nelson, Collingwood and Cockburn,
the Letters and Journals of Major T.M. Wybourn,
ed. Anne Petrides and Jonathan Downs
Humanity Dick, the Story of Richard Martin pioneer of Animal Rights,
by Peter Phillips

By the same author, available from Parapress:
Change at Peckham Rye, and other stories

First edition published 1994
New paperback edition June 2001
Reprinted October 2001
This edition printed 2010

ISBN-10: 1-898594-70-8
ISBN-13: 978-1-898594-70-3

PARAPRESS LTD
The Basement
9 Frant Road
Tunbridge Wells
Kent
TN2 5SD UK
www.parapress.co.uk

British Library Cataloguing in Publication Data:
a catalogue record for this book is available from the British Library.

Cover design by Mousemat Design Ltd
www.mousematdesign.com

Tyypeset by Vitaset, Paddock Wood, Kent

Printed and bound by
The Berforts Group
www.berforts.com

Print management by Sutherland Eve Production, Tunbridge Wells, Kent
guyeve@theeves.fsnet.co.uk

To the Ganavan Wrens

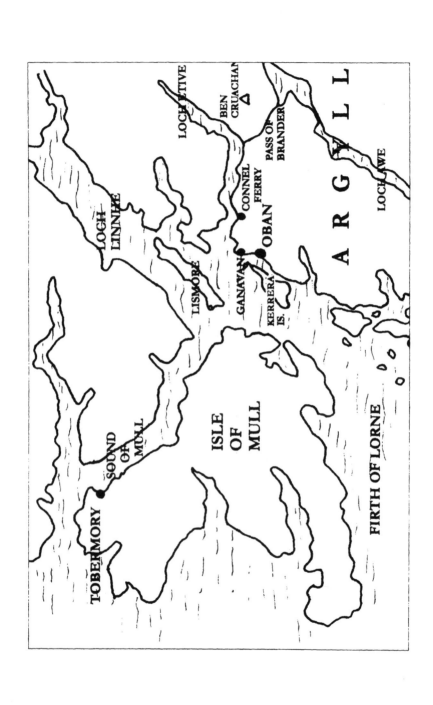

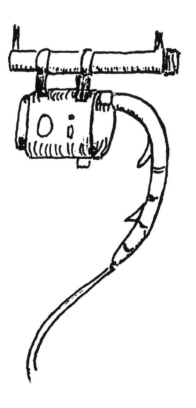

Aldis lamp

I

The Melting Pot

1

V/S

'You'll never get in the Wrens,' my friends said. 'They're awfully choosey. They only take girls who've got relations who are naval officers. And they've all been to Roedean.'

'You'll be terribly homesick,' my family said. 'You've never been away from home at all. And what will happen about airing your clothes and drying your hair properly – you know what frightful colds you get.'

'But what on earth *for*,' they said at work. 'You're in a reserved occupation. You can stay here for the rest of the war.'

That was what I was afraid of.

I had done nine months' secretarial training, but of course I wouldn't be a real secretary for years and years. I was a junior dogsbody – a runner of errands and messages.

At Guy's hospital where I worked, I collected the admission books from the wards each morning. The ambulant patients from the previous night's bombing, swathed in bloodstained bandages or with their burnt hands and faces horrifically painted mauve with gentian violet, were already being stuffed into coaches for the journey down to the Sector hospitals in Kent. I entered the patients' names in a huge leather-bound book I could only just lift, and wrote out bed-cards and took them back to the wards. Then I fetched a big china jug of coffee from the kitchen block for the elevenses of my superiors. After that I sat at a counter by the Brought in Dead list.

During a night raid, if bodies brought in dead could be identified, their names were scrawled in pencil on a list, on the way to the mortuary. In the morning, a poignant little queue formed of people who had clawed their way out of the rubble and couldn't find their relations who had been harmlessly eating sandwiches with them when the bomb fell. The list was long and not alphabetical and often had a bloodstained thumbprint on the top page. If I found a name resembling the one they asked for, they had to be taken to the mortuary to see the pieces.

I wore a pale green overall with dark green collar and cuffs, and an enamel badge saying Hospital Emergency Service, of which I was very proud, and I had a black cape with a scarlet lining, like the nurses. I used to come down the steps from the kitchen and across the open to the administrative block with my cape swirling and the coffee jug held carefully between my two hands, the steam rising in fragrant waves. As I crunched my way through broken glass, stepping over the previous night's hoses which the blear-eyed firemen were trying to coil up for the next night, with the smell of smoke hanging in the air, the job seemed to me to have a certain panache. But it was not enough to satisfy me.

After lunch in the Nurses' Home I used to scurry up on to London Bridge and lean over and snuff up the pungent smell of London river, which is one of the best smells in the world, and gaze at the ships, and dream, and dream: an impossible dream of Getting on a Boat. The only boat I had ever been on was a launch called the *Condor* which took holidaymakers round the harbour at Lyme Regis in August 1938.

In the afternoons I typed the weekly wages sheets. As I unhooked the short carriage from the typewriter and hooked on the long carriage, a depression like cold porridge used to settle over me. I tore off a batch of ruled sheets, inserted the large oblongs of carbon paper, and started down the long, long list of porters, wardmaids and cooks, of whom there were hundreds. Once a month there were all the nurses as well. The figures were all written out and added up by hand by the Wages Clerk, who was worried and elderly and had dedicated her whole life to wages, and the tabulating was as intricate as a typing exam.

I could never understand figures, and one week I typed a whole page on the wrong line and sent all the wages haywire. While I was cringing outside the door, I heard the Wages Clerk say to the Finance Officer, 'It's that bloody girl again, if you ask me she's half-witted, she's no right to be employed in a place like this.'

At that moment I realised the joke had gone on long enough and whatever I had to do to avoid it, I wasn't going to be there to receive a silver coffee-pot on my sixtieth birthday.

It was time to stop dreaming.

'But why?' the hospital people said. 'Why leave a really well paid job, £120 a year, and just go and type the same sort of lists for £1 a week?' I could sympathise. I was a sort of reproach to them, an implied aspersion on their indispensability.

'I'm not going to type,' I said.

I had been seduced by a leaflet given to me by a school friend who had joined the Wrens as a Wireless Telegraphist. The leaflet was about a Signal School in Lancashire called HMS *Cabbala*, where they trained Wireless Telegraphists, Coders, and Visual Signallers. As soon as I saw the photographs of girls signalling with lamps and doing semaphore and hoisting flags up masts, I knew that was what I was going to do, and nothing else.

Even the school friend tried to put me off. 'The signallers were out in all weathers when I was there,' she said. 'They were blue with cold, they got pneumonia. Why don't you do W/T and be in a nice cosy nissen hut? You know how you hated games at school.'

It was true. The worst misery of my life was enduring squelching about on a tilted balding field in a north-east wind with someone shouting, 'Run girl, can't you!'

I said, 'I shall go there in the summer then.'

Towards the end of 1942 I asked at work if I could leave a bit early one evening to go to the dentist. I went to Westminster, to the WRNS Recruiting Office. There was a poster in the window, of a healthy, smiling, apple-cheeked girl with dark springing hair, in Wren uniform, with flags in the background. It said, 'Join the Wrens and Free a Man for the Fleet.'

When I had worked up the queue, across a trestle table I surveyed a woman in uniform jacket with buttons on the cuffs. She didn't look glowing like the girl on the poster, and neither did I. We both looked pasty. We spent all our evenings and nights down the shelter.

I said, 'I want to be a visual signaller.'

'Sorry,' she said. 'I'm afraid that category is closed and there's a waiting list. I doubt if we shall recruit any more. At the moment the only categories open are Writers and Cooks. Can you do shorthand and typing?'

'No,' I said.

'What a pity,' she said. 'Well, just fill in the form and where it says "category" put "cook". I'm sure you like cooking, don't you?'

'No,' I said. 'I hate it.'

I took the form home and where it said 'category' I put 'Visual

5

Signaller', and where it said 'second choice' I put 'none' and I posted it back.

Three weeks later a buff card came with an Admiralty stamp requesting my presence for an eye test at the Naval Recruiting Office in Charing Cross Road. Twelve of us sat in silence in a waiting room eyeing each other curiously. Suddenly one girl burst out, 'I'm *sure* they won't take me, I wear glasses; I shall *die* if I don't get in.'

We looked at cards of letters, in dark rooms we looked at lights, we looked at pictures of dots with figures hidden in them; men in white coats peered into our eyes, they asked us about headaches and migraine, and we were shunted out on to the pavement in a state of anguished uncertainty. We were already a group. I could see a consuming passion in their faces which I knew was in mine too; the spirit of Nelson and Jellicoe had possessed us. 'Goodbye, goodbye,' we all said, 'perhaps we'll meet again.'

Only one, a dark girl like the one on the poster, in a pink jacket, gave a confident grin and shouted 'See you all at *Cabbala!* What *fun* it'll be!'

Two weeks later I got a postcard telling me I had passed the eye test, and inviting me to a medical at the local Labour Exchange. I jumped the gun and started having inoculations and vaccinations at the hospital. In March I hopefully gave notice, and spent the last week typing for the Dean of the Medical School, surrounded by jars of two-headed foetuses in formaldehyde.

A clothing list arrived: pyjamas, dressing gown, rug, shorts, gym shoes. My family rallied round with coupons. 'Don't forget,' they said, 'you can still come out after the first fortnight if you don't like it, you're a probationer for two weeks.' They didn't actually advise me to boil all the drinking water and sleep under a mosquito net, because nobody in our acquaintance had ever been abroad in those days. As they knew, if I did come out after a fortnight, having left a reserved occupation, I would be snapped up at once by the ATS or the WAAF. I had nothing against the ATS or the WAAF except that they didn't have telescopes, and generally lacked the special glamour of the Navy.

On 25 May, a nice warm summer day, I got the Manchester train from Euston with my friend Dorothy. Our mothers saw us off. By that time we had, metaphorically, very cold feet, and a mental picture of a camp in Lancashire like the salt mines in Siberia. Neither of us had ever been so far from home before.

At school, I had observed Dorothy to be one of life's experts in the art of passive resistance to Authority. Never Absent, Never Late was the cardinal precept of the Headmistress. Dorothy had always been late. Her lateness was a demonstration of the art of lateness. She would slide in at the back, raising a faintly quizzical eyebrow, as though to indicate 'How foolish of them, to start this class twenty minutes early without telling me.' As for absent – she was not often physically absent, but most of the time, especially when being told to do something, Dorothy was indubitably mentally absent. If one did not notice the rare flash of a surprisingly alert blue eye, and the rather mulish set of the jaw, one might have thought that Dorothy was not really capable of absorbing knowledge.

I had the feeling that the Navy wouldn't get the better of Dorothy, any more than school had. She was not mouldable. We had struggled into gym tunics and felt hats and panama hats together – now we would struggle into bellbottoms and white shirts and round caps together, but still we would reserve judgement about keeping the rules.

The travel warrant said 'Manchester, London Road', but when we got there the RTO office told us we would have to get a taxi to Manchester Exchange for a train to Lowton St Mary's where the camp was.

There was another girl in the RTO office being directed to Manchester Exchange, a large bronzed girl with very black eyes and a heap of luggage. Feeling I was becoming quite cosmopolitan, I said rather patronisingly to her, 'Have you come far?' In a deep gloomy voice she replied, 'Frum Brassil.' After a silence she added, 'Via New York.'

The three of us shared a taxi for three shillings to Manchester Exchange, where a porter greeted us with, 'Nay lass, 'tis wrong station: you want Manchester Central.' As our second taxi was starting up the door was wrenched open and someone else fell in on top of a case.

'Oh!' I said, 'the girl with glasses!'

'Yes,' she gasped, 'they took me, wasn't it smashing, I'd have *died* if they hadn't.'

7

From Manchester Central the train had little compartments with hard, upright seats and pictures of Blackpool behind our heads, and went slowly through flat fields towards Warrington. We seemed the only four people going anywhere through the warm afternoon.

'Lowton St Mary's,' a porter shouted. We came to a stop at a country halt, very clean, with bright flowers in a bed edged with whitewashed stones. Doors were opening all down the train, and girls dragging cases down onto the platform.

'Look,' I said to Dorothy, 'there's the girl in the pink jacket.'

There was also a Wren Petty Officer waving us along towards a group of young sailors with handcarts for the luggage. We walked over the lane to the camp. The sun was out, sailors with fixed bayonets were guarding the gates, there was a huge ship's bell, and inside the gateway the White Ensign was fluttering. There were wide concrete paths bordered by neat flowerbeds, well built single-storey huts set back each side, everyone was smiling, and suddenly I knew it was going to be all right. For once I had done the right thing.

I had also learnt not to take too much notice of what other people say.

2

HMS *Cabbala*

HMS *Cabbala* was an ex-Ministry of Supply hutted camp, which had been built for factory workers and taken over by the Navy in 1942 as the first Combined Signal School where Wren Wireless Telegraphists, Visual Signallers and Coders were trained, 400 at a time. Naval ratings were also trained there in the same three branches of Communications. The accommodation was far superior to anything purpose-built for the WRNS – better equipped and more spacious. By the time I got there the rooms designed for two factory workers were each holding three Wrens, with a double bunk and a single bed, but even so they were very comfortable, and the common rooms and ablution blocks were luxurious compared with any the Navy was able to provide.

About forty of us had arrived at Lowton St Mary's station together, of whom twenty-four were destined to be V/S. The youngest was seventeen, and the oldest was twenty-three. We were dispersed among the H-shaped huts, each of which accommodated ninety-four Wrens in cabins off each side of corridors down the legs of the H, with ablution blocks, and a Common Room with a wireless and gramophone, in the crosspiece.

Dorothy and I were deposited at Block M of Camp 31, and told to find Cabin 23, where the occupant of the single bed would initiate us into life in double bunks. When we opened the door a wave of smoke wafted out and an irritable voice said, 'Shut it quickly, for God's sake.'

Lying on the single bed, wearing a Wren skirt and shirt with an RAF silk scarf knotted in the neck was someone willowy, with a Veronica Lake hairdo – ash blonde, straightish, side parting, with a curtain falling over one eye. Her visible eye scowled and went back to the paperback propped up on her stomach, which was called *Dames in Love and War* and had on the cover a picture of a girl in bra and pants sitting on the torch of the Statue of Liberty.

'Roberta,' she drawled. 'So you've joined the Navy.' She waved a hand with scarlet nails towards the double bunk. A charm bracelet jingled. 'It's all yours. One drawer each and two inches in the hanging cupboard.' With an undulating movement she rose from the bed, planted a smacking kiss on the large framed photograph on the chest of drawers, and went out, saying over her shoulder, 'You can each put a photo on the chest, but don't move my sweetie-pie. See you.'

As the door closed we looked at each other and then at her sweetie-pie. He had crinkly fair hair and a rather thin neck, and was in naval officer's uniform. I tried not to encourage the unworthy thought that he was probably only a Sub-Lieutenant, otherwise he would have rested his chin on his hand to show the stripes on his sleeve. Across the photo was scrawled in schoolboy writing, 'To darling Roberta, always and for ever, love and kisses from your own Denny.'

I flung the window open. 'That nice Wren who brought us round, the officer or Petty Officer or whoever she was, said we mustn't smoke in the cabins,' I said.

We squashed our clothes into one drawer each. Dorothy said thoughtfully, 'I don't think Roberta's a new Wren at all.'

'Why?'

'Well, did you notice, she's got a zip in her skirt, and it fits. That lot we passed on the way in, who were marching in shirts and skirts, their skirts had a sort of placket one side of the stomach with buttons, all bunchy looking.'

There was a bang on the door and someone shouted, 'Supper on the Mess Deck.' We joined the rush of feet up the corridor.

The Mess Deck was the largest hall I had ever been in, filled with rows and rows of wooden tables and wooden benches. There were plates of cut bread on each table, and a high pile of bowls at one end. The noise was unbelievable.

When we had all squeezed in, the stewards came bursting out of the galley at a gallop and banged down a steel cauldron with a ladle at the end of each table. The two Wrens at the top started to ladle out the unrecognisable contents and slither them down to the end in bowls. Before the ones at the end had got their portions the stewards were on the gallop back, swinging up the cauldrons in passing.

They were overtaken by a second lot, banging a pile of smaller bowls down on the end of each table, and a smaller cauldron containing a recognisable if emaciated form of rice pudding. On their return trip to collect these, a whistle sounded and a voice over the tannoy quacked, 'Newly joined recruits, lecture from Chief Officer in Lecture Hall 10, in two minutes.'

The lecture was brisk, stimulating and informative. As the Chief Officer went out, a Petty Officer got to her feet. 'Now I'll take you to the canteen for cocoa. Then bed. Up at 0700, clean your cabins before breakfast, breakfast at 0800, then Divisions, then march at the double to the classroom for your first lecture.' She suddenly relaxed and smiled. 'I hope you'll enjoy it and be happy. If there's anything you want to know, please come and ask me.' She went out, and we followed.

'She's the crusher, Regulating PO,' said the girl next to me, sipping cocoa. 'What did yer do before yer joined up?'

'Clerk in a hospital,' I said. 'What did you?'

'Woolworfs, Balham High Road,' she said with a grin. 'Lectrical counter. I'm doing W/T. Me bruvver's a sparks. At Pompey.' I didn't know where Pompey was. It sounded foreign.

The girl the other side said, 'I was a teacher till yesterday.'

'Where?' I asked.

'A village in Anglesey. Miss Williams will have come back today to take over. I wonder how she'll get on. She's nearly seventy.' Her voice was soft and lilting. She said, 'My fiancé was killed. On the *Hunter*, at Narvik. He was a teacher too. I couldn't just do nothing.'

Into the melting pot we all went – conscripts, volunteers, engaged, married, widowed, single, Zara from Brazil, Rita from Balham, Cathy from Anglesey, Marianne from Barclays Bank in Aberdeen, Joy from Sainsbury's cold meat counter in Birmingham, Clodagh from milking her father's cows near Kinsale in County Cork, Maureen from being a hotel chambermaid in Dublin – Dublin that still had bright lights and butter and a German Embassy – Jane from helping her mother run a boarding house in Skegness, Judy straight from school, Pauline from an estate agent's in Wood Green, Celia from the Prudential in Exeter, Vivienne, a second year nurse at Leeds General Infirmary, Patricia from a repertory company in Belfast, Betty who thought life was fun, Irene who wore glasses.

None of us had fathers or brothers who were naval officers, and

I guessed that a lot of us had left school at fourteen. Our clothes were different from one another's and our accents were different and our backgrounds were different. We only shared one thing in common – our dreams. We had almost all spent every Saturday afternoon of our youth at the pictures, with Clark Gable and Cary Grant and Leslie Howard and Fred Astaire and Gary Cooper and Tyrone Power. That was our common denominator, and it rosily coloured our expectations for the future.

Four weeks later, out of the melting pot came the coders; sixteen weeks later the V/S's; and six months later the W/T's; not yet looking like the girl on the poster but, give or take a few bumps, looking roughly the same size and shape. The prototype Wren, knowing that Pompey was Portsmouth, and gash meant redundant, and slops was stores, and chokker was fed-up, and rabbiting was thieving, and a bottle was a row, and a stand-easy bun was elevenses, and a gannet was greedy, and Jimmy the One was the First Lieutenant, and tiddley was for best, and to put the anchor on the bedspread the right way up or the ship would sink. We had entered the only real democracy. We weren't pretending to be equal: we *were* equal, and might have to go on being equal for years and years. It was a great relief.

Yet inside the buttoned jackets and under the round caps, which looked so identical, were separate seething, bubbling cauldrons of emotion – patriotism, desire to win the war, pride in the Navy, confidence in the training we had received, belief that ours was the best job in the world, hunger for food and hunger for male company, and the sentimental mishmash of daydreams which had also shaped our youthful minds.

Back in the cabin, Dorothy and I yawned at each other. We got into our new sensible striped pyjamas. I hauled myself up into the top bunk and strapped my watch round the metal frame.

Roberta looked up from her paperback. She was wearing a pink satin nightie with blue ribbons threaded round the low neck. 'So what are you?' she asked. 'Bunts or sparks?'

'Visual signallers,' Dorothy said.

'Ha! Bunting tossers,' she said. 'You'll learn all the rude signals.'

'How long have you been in?' I asked her.

'Two flaming years,' she said.

'Gosh – ever since 1941.'

12

'Remustered as a coder, to get overseas. Only way of getting out of this blasted country. Another two weeks to go in this dump.'

'Where have you been stationed up to now?'

'Plymouth. I was an Immobile – lived at home. OK while my sweetie-pie was there. One of you's got to get out and switch off the light.' She turned her back and hunched the bedclothes over her shoulder.

Dorothy gave me a look which I took to mean, 'We can stick anything for two weeks,' and slid out of bed.

3

Pro-Wrens

Being a Pro-Wren meant chores. Dorothy's alarm went at 0700. We sprang out of bed conscientiously, got dressed, discovered the broom cupboard, and started sweeping out the cabin. The floors were all pitchmastic. As we scooped out fluff from under Roberta's bed, she came up on one elbow, lit a cigarette, surveyed us in a forbearing way and said, 'What *dear* little housewives you two will make.'

The procedure for breakfast was less satisfactory than that for supper. At the end of each table the stewards dumped a metal canister of cornflakes, a steel jug of watered milk, a smaller canister of sugar, and a pile of bowls. The cornflakes canister filled the first ten bowls. The milk and sugar filled the first six. The rest of us did without. We had already entered the law of the jungle, and from now on we were always so hungry that we were incapable of considering one another. If you didn't get a place near the top of the table you went without.

When we got back to the cabin Roberta was still in bed, eating biscuits. I conceded that she had a point.

I said, 'Is there a shop near, where I can buy a tooth mug?'

'You must be out of your tiny wits,' said Roberta. 'What do you think the things in the Mess Deck are for if not to nick?' She pulled open a drawer. Under her pants were three glasses, six plates, and a handful of cutlery. She handed me a glass. 'Have a rabbit,' she said.

We all went to Sick Bay and had our heads searched. A few were detained and had to report back every morning to have their hair washed. They used to slide in at the back of the lecture hut with crimson faces and hair dripping on the desk. The charitable legend was spread that 'they must have caught them on the train from Manchester'.

We packed away our jumpers and skirts and silk stockings and court shoes, and put on bluettes and lisle stockings. Bluettes would have looked at home in a penal settlement. They were designed expressly to make you pack in the whole daft idea and go home before your probationary fortnight was over. They were boiled-out blue overall dresses of a kind of sponge cloth, buttoning up to the neck. Worn without slips, they rucked up in front, sticking to our stockings as we walked. All that was missing was the arrows.

When we were on Long Watch duty, I knelt in my rucked-up bluette at one end of one of the long-leg corridors, and over my shoulder I could just see Dorothy's kneeling feet about half a mile away up the other end. We scrubbed silently and industriously nearer until the soles of our feet touched an hour later. I thought it was marvellous; much better than typing wages sheets.

The next morning when the alarm went I said, 'Aren't you on Long Watch, Roberta?'

'So what?' she said.

'PO Blundell said you missed it last time – she'd make you scrub both corridors if you didn't report today.'

'Lot of sex-starved old maids,' muttered Roberta. She turned over and went to sleep again.

Ten minutes later Jane burst in. 'You needn't think I'm doing it alone again, so there!' she shouted, dragging the clothes off Roberta.

'Just you wait,' hissed Roberta. 'Just you wait until *you've* been in two years, until you are sick, sick, sick of it all: looking alike, saying the same things, thinking the same things, until you could scream and scream –.'

We gaped at her. We couldn't imagine a time when we weren't bending all our powers towards being exactly like everybody else who was our age.

The SanitaryTowel run at *Cabbala* had become quite famous. I had heard about it long before I joined up. On ST duty morning you had to spread sheets of newspaper all over the lavatory floor and tip the contents of the bins on to it. There were a lot, with ninety-four Wrens in a block. You then had to make a rough parcel, hoping it wouldn't be too large and unwieldy to carry hugged to your chest and you wouldn't have to come back a second time. You were wise to do it up fairly securely, because you and the parcel had to proceed right through the Wren camp, right through the sailors' camp, to the boiler house on the perimeter

15

fence at the far side, where you handed it to a scarlet-faced rating. Your eyes and his were riveted to the ground between your feet. The chanting voices of the sailors wafted on the air – 'You don't have to tell us, we know ....'

We did Mess Duty. This involved clearing tea and laying supper for 1,000, and helping to wash up after supper. Washing up went on for about two hours, in a temperature of 81°F and a noise so frightful that even if you shouted at the top of your voice into someone's ear they could not hear you. It was designed to stop you in your tracks if, ever after, you felt like criticising a cook or a steward.

The floor of the galley was about two inches deep in slopping liquid, in which cabbage leaves, tea-leaves, bread, potato peelings and porridge floated. There was a drain in the middle which was blocked up. About a hundred ratings, stripped to the waist, were hurling cauldrons, frying pans, teapots, saucepans and cutlery over your head. One of them seized your hand, put into it a sodden string of cloth, and pointed wordlessly to a pile of plates starting under water on the floor and reaching far above your head. You started wiping and wiping and wiping, fruitlessly as the cloth was sopping wet. There were fifty more piles of plates behind you. You held out the sopping rag to the nearest sailor. He slung it round the table leg, wound it tight to wring out the surplus, and handed it back to you. After the first hour you felt that you had never done anything but wipe plates.

When it was over you found you were stone deaf for twenty minutes. Your friends helped you out of your spattered bluette and into a bath. They were shouting something. 'Congratulations – you didn't faint. People usually do, the first time.'

I still thought life was marvellous.

When you were Watch Leader, at the end of a day of Long Watch duty you had to inspect the whole hut, and then sit and wait in the Common Room for the Duty Officer. When she appeared you leapt up, switched off the wireless, sprang to attention and said, 'All present and correct, Ma'am.' The first time Celia did this she went back into the ablutions when the officer had gone and found that a water tank had burst and a sizeable river was running down the corridor.

We were all issued with identity discs, in case we were blown up or drowned, though neither fate seemed very likely at HMS *Cabbala*. They were of some pinkish, indestructible substance, and had our name and religion stamped on. We hung them round our necks on pieces of string, and wrote home asking if our mothers had still got that old silver chain Granny used to wear. We did PT and we played rounders. We had a lecture on security. We went to an ENSA concert.

We weren't allowed to speak to the sailors in the camp. Dorothy and I went out of camp for the first time one evening and walked over a meadow intersected by overgrown ditches. The landscape appeared deserted, but after a time we could hear rustlings and scufflings all round us from sailors and Wrens clasped in each other's arms in any patch of cover. It was a mystery how they had made the initial contact.

There was a dance once a week in the big hall. All the sailors stood up one end and all the Wrens the other. The band played,

> The sweetest song in the world is sung
> When you're in love and your heart is young,
> We sang it together in the twilight glow,
> Not so very long ago, do you recall ...

The Captain, who was white-haired and venerable and looked like Owen Nares, came in and rattled his stick along the thin legs of the sailors as if they were railings, shouting, '*Dance* with the gels you lads, *dance* with the gels!' at which they bent their heads, wrung their hands in an agony of bashfulness, and backed out of the doors.

> For it is love and love alone will bring to you
> The sweetest song in the world.

But they had all gone.

On Sunday we had a march past and Church Parade. We all filed into the same huge hall and sang hymns to a Marine band. At the end of the Service, the sailors sang 'For those in peril on the sea'. Our futile female trebles faded out as their young male voices rose and fell like the waves in that saddest and most majestic of all hymns. Suddenly we saw them not as adolescent

17

garage hands and bank clerks and shop assistants, with pimples and Adam's apples dressed up in eighteenth-century fancy dress, but as endowed with all the drama, the bravery and endurance and humour and pageantry and gallantry of 'they that go down to the sea in ships and occupy their business in great waters.' Lumps came into our throats. That is a hymn for men to sing and for women to weep to.

4

Signals

Betty burst into the cabin. 'Have you *seen* our instructor? Oh gosh, he's smashing – he looks just like John Clements! Awfully young. All the other V/S instructors are ancient, and the W/T instructors are all women, so aren't we *lucky?*'

Indeed we were. Chief Petty Officer Brown was on short shore leave following an injury. He was so handsome, and so enthusiastic and keen to teach us, that we all fell in love with him on the first day.

'You're going to learn morse until it comes out of your ears,' he said. 'You're going to think in morse. You won't be able to speak except in dots and dashes. When you walk along the road you'll look at the hoardings and read all the advertisements in morse. And you're going to signal morse faster than any girls have ever signalled it before.' And so we did.

For hours we sat chanting, 'Dah-dit-dit – dance on it – D; dah-dit-dah-dit – cat and kittens – C; dah-dah-dit-dah – God Save the Queen – Q; dit-dit-dah-dit – if you funk it – F.'

'And if you don't know SOS and V you can pack up and go home now,' he added.

The classes were haunted by the Training Commander RNVR (who looked like Clive Brook) known as Old Snoopy, who kept peering in through the glass fanlight, obviously certain that no good could come of putting such a heavenly man in charge of all those nubile girls. 'What the devil,' Old Snoopy prefixed all his remarks, 'What the devil are you doing, Brown, taking a two-week test after one week's instruction?'

'They've all passed, sir,' said Chief meekly.

No wonder, when all the signals he sent us to read were about camp personalities. 'Who do you think Third Officer Bates was out with last night?' the slow accurate morse flashed out in the first lesson of the day. 'And what time she came in?' We were rapt, avid for more.

'You don't want to take any notice of Old Snoopy,' said Chief scornfully. 'He's only Wavy Navy. I never salute the RNVR if I can help it – I blow my nose or sneeze as I pass them.'

Fortunately his strictures passed unheeded. To us a naval officer was a naval officer was a man, whether his stripes were straight or wavy, and if they were wavy perhaps he needed our respect even more because, like us, he wasn't real Navy and for most of the time he hadn't a clue what he was supposed to be doing or why.

The only person Chief respected was the Signal Bo'sun, nick-named Dracula, an embittered character with a sarcastic tongue and a phenomenal knowledge of all things appertaining to signalling, who was unwillingly confined to a shore job on medical grounds.

Beginning to think in morse, out we trooped to the parade ground. It was warm and sunny. 'Spread out!' roared Chief, 'in pairs!' Off we went to the far corners, one facing him to read, the other with back turned to write down. Semaphore this morning. 'The Lieutenant from the Admiralty who lectured to you last night on Security and was introduced as an old *Cabbala*-ite, failed his coder exams and was chucked out.' We fell about laughing.

He looked so neat doing semaphore, his arms moving effortlessly into the right positions with a flick of the wrist. It was poetry in motion, almost as good as ballet, which was the highest praise I could give. When we tried we became hysterical. We sawed our arms about. Somehow our bosoms got in the way and the flags never went into the angles we meant them to. Our bluettes started to split under the arms. Our biceps ached with the strain.

'You there, Thompson, what was that letter you just read to your oppo?'

'A, Chief.'

'A? A? What's A? It doesn't exist. A what?'

'Apples, Chief.'

'It's *not* Apples any more girl, how many more times, it's Abel now, we're with the Yanks – go on now, all of you, say it again –.'

'Abel, Baker, Charlie, Delta,' we chanted. The phonetic alphabet had just been changed.

'You'd better know it well,' said Chief. 'The sooner you do, the sooner I'll have you reading in words, not letters.'

20

Back to the classroom for a lecture on ranks and badges and saluting. They told us about Captains and First Lieutenants, but they didn't tell us that shore-based Captains were elderly and grizzled and venerable and white-haired, and that First Lieutenants were often randy and had Wrens' bras and panties airing in front of their office fires.

Out on the parade ground again. We gathered round a large grey lamp on a fixed stand. 'This is the ten-inch,' shouted Chief. 'Because it measures ten inches across the shutter. Behind the shutter is a lamp. When you push the handle on the right up and down, the shutter goes up and down and the light is blocked off in dots and dashes.' The ten-inch was never a favourite. It was slow and cumbersome and clanking to use.

Chief took a little lamp, attached by a long lead to a battery, in his hand. 'This will be your first love,' he said. 'It has a reflector behind the lamp. Your forefinger tilts the reflector and sends the beam focusing on the ship you are signalling to. It's light and very fast.'

We held the lamp in turn. 'Now I'll teach you flashing,' he said, 'and by the time I've finished, the men on the ships you signal to will think they're signalling to another *man* in the signal station.'

Flashing hadn't a debased meaning then. It meant sending morse by light over the sea. As I cupped the Aldis in my left hand, put my forefinger on the trigger, and my other fingers on the lamp switch, and my right eye to the half-perished stiff grey rubber telescopic eye-piece, what he said came true. I fell in love with the Aldis lamp, as I knew I would. In my hand I had ultimate power over the Navy. I could say to a battleship five miles away, 'Turn round and go back again,' and it would obediently do so.

'Keep your left eye open,' said Chief, 'otherwise you'll go paralysed after the first hour or two.'

We went back to the classroom for a lecture on ship recognition. My first notebook was full already. In the evenings we lay on our bunks tapping out morse to each other on the metal frame.

'Do you know,' said Dorothy, 'we've been here two whole weeks?'

'Then Roberta goes tomorrow!' we both said together.

'Where is Roberta? It's after eleven.'

'Perhaps she got a late pass.'

'She can't have gone because Sweetie-pie is still here.' There was an Air Mail letter propped up in front of Sweetie-pie. We put the light out and lay down. We usually went off like logs until the alarm went, but this time we were restless. I woke up with a jerk. I could see in the faint light from the fanlight over the door that it was 1.0 – in fact 0100 as we called it. The blackout curtain suddenly bulged in front of the open window and a long slender leg clad in black silk stocking crept cautiously over the sill. A wedge of bright moonlight came quietly in with Roberta.

Dorothy and I each watched her through a crack of eyelid. She stood in front of the mirror and lit a cigarette, her eyes on her reflection. She started to sing very softly,

'Moonlight becomes you,
It goes with your hair ...'

As she sang she slipped off her jacket and dropped it on the floor.

'You certainly know the right thing to wear ...'

Slowly she unzipped her skirt, let it fall, and stepped out of it. Immediately the image changed. In her shirt, which almost covered her buttocks, her suspenders and long black stockings, she looked titillating, like the cover of *Reveille*.

She blew a slow smoke ring at her reflection.

'When I say I love you,
I want you to know ...'

Her voice was husky, intimate. She kicked off her shoes, rolled down her stockings, and flexed her long slender feet. Then she dragged off her tie, threw it on the bed, and ripped the buttons of her shirt undone. Underneath she was wearing a bra and a minute suspender belt.

'It's not just because there's moonlight, although ...'

Roberta slowly unhooked the bra and the belt and dropped them to the floor. She stood in front of the mirror, naked except for her hat.

'Moonlight becomes you so.'

Her image was printed for ever on my memory. Her flesh was so flawless that it seemed a gasp would have shattered it. I knew I didn't look like that, and never would. It was not just the full moons of her breasts, her taut stomach, the pale column of her throat, the firmness of her thighs. It was the proudness of her stance. What did it feel like, I wondered, to be so at home in your body, so sure of its power and potential?

Roberta gave a final drag at her cigarette and stubbed it out on her sweetie-pie's kisser. 'Ha,' she said on a short, sharp, savage note. She put the photograph frame face down and sprang into bed, hat and all.

I leant over the edge of the top bunk. I could see Dorothy's eyes wide with horrified disapproval.

The next day Roberta was drafted, and we got our uniform, and Ruth came.

5

Kitting Up

For the last time, we put on the abysmal bluettes. This was the great day for which we had been waiting so long. Now we should look like the girl on the poster.

We filed into a very long narrow hut with a counter stretching down its length and shelves from floor to ceiling behind. As we moved along, the Leading Wrens behind the counter started dumping a pile of clothing in front of each of us.

Two skirts and two jackets, a tiddley one and an everyday one; two pairs of 'blackouts', i.e. knickers, navy artificial silk, and down to the knee; two pairs of black lisle stockings; two pairs of shoes, a raincoat, a greatcoat, a tie. Six collars, two sizes too large because they would shrink in the laundry. Six shirts, the right size because they wouldn't. Between the back stud and the front stud there was always a bulge of collar over shirt. The collars did shrink, but before they were down to shirt size they got so worn that they rubbed our necks raw even when we put candle grease on. The hat, the crowning glory! A taffeta hat ribbon with 'H.M.S.' worked in gold on it. And, because we would work outdoors, two pairs of thick navy woollen blackouts, two pairs of bellbottoms, a seaman's jersey, and woollen gloves and socks.

We tottered back clasping our burdens, and about ten of us piled into Betty's cabin. 'Look at these woollen knickers!' shrieked Jane. 'Just imagine anyone thinking we would be seen dead in them!' We all packed them up and sent them to our elderly aunts, who were delighted. By about November, standing about on cliffs in the Hebrides, we would have given anything to have them back.

The skirts had the curious placket we had noticed, with large buttons. When we put them on we looked as if we had hernias. On some of us they reached the ankles and on some of us they were up to the thighs. They all had to be the correct number of inches off the ground before we were allowed out of camp. We ironed the panel seams to look like pleats.

The jackets had an inner pocket over the left breast. We had to keep our pay books there. With a hernia on the hip and a flattened breast on the left we had a decidedly lopsided appearance. We struggled into the raincoats. Over the jackets they made us look square. We tried them without jackets and pulled in the belt very tightly. We thought that those of us who had waists looked simply wizard. It was a pity about the others. You couldn't get the greatcoat on and done up over a jacket, if you did you looked rather like a ship's fender, but presumably you wouldn't want to. We could hardly lift the greatcoats anyway – they would have stood up without us.

There was something wrong about the hat. It looked like a pancake. 'I'll show you what to do,' said Cathy. 'My cabin mate told me. You make a roll of newspaper and put it round the brim inside to make it stand up.'

Patricia said, 'They have tiddley bows in the ribbon, with a sixpence in them. How can we get those?'

'Don't worry, I'll get round Chief,' Betty said. Poor Chief – we gave him ribbons and sixpences and he made twenty-four tiddley bows for us. Betty could get round anyone. She was stocky, dominant, determined, with black eyes and black hair and gypsy looks. She was invulnerable, and she magnetised us into doing what she wanted.

The only thing that didn't need altering was the seaman's jersey. It was perfect. It came down to our knees. It was warm and comfortable and indestructible. It could be boiled, scorched, scrubbed, slept in, lived in, and would last a lifetime.

That left the *pièce de résistance*, the bellbottoms. They were our badge of office, our passport to a man's job, and in them we intended to swank around the camps and bases of the future with our bottoms cheekily outlined and our waists nipped in. Alas, a shattering blow awaited us. They were folded inside out, because the crease each side had to go inwards. There seemed a lot of blue and white striped ticking round the waist, with layers of wadding. When we pulled them right way out we were appalled.

'They're not for Wrens – they're sailors' bellbottoms,' said Maureen, shocked.

Sailors' bellbottoms were three flaps thick over the stomach, of the best stout serge. Two of the flaps were sturdily lined with ticking – one came from each side and they buttoned together down the middle. Over them a third flap lifted up and buttoned to each side seam. It was true that they were tight over the seat, but on us the flaps stuck out over our stomachs in an obscene way. The sailors' jumpers decently covered all the flaps, and men's stomachs are flatter anyway, but we had to wear them with white shirts tucked in.

'We can't wear them like this,' moaned Marianne, peering down the large gap between her waist and the top flap, as though expecting to find a baby kangaroo there.

Celia was already on her knees with safety pins in her mouth. She was the class leader – a calm, placid girl with classic features, a born mediator. 'We'll have to cut off the side flaps and just pray they hold together,' she said decisively. 'Until we go on leave, and our mothers can alter them.' So like generations at *Cabbala* before us, we did. Without the side flaps they weren't quite so laughable, but the awful truth was that kitted up we did all look like nothing so much as Tom Kitten.

Dorothy and I, in new shirts and skirts, dragged the unwieldy piles back to our cabin. We hung as much as we could in the hanging cupboard, which was a small triangular piece of plywood, nailed across one corner, with a cretonne curtain hanging down in front, and the rest had to go in our suitcases.

There was a knock on the door and in came a girl in a blue linen skirt and a pink blouse. She had very fine mousey hair which fell over her forehead in a soft fringe. Her eyes were brown and took in us and the cabin with one swift appraisal.

'Hallo,' she said, 'I'm Ruth. I think I'm in here.'

'Oh gosh,' I said, 'we ought to have seen if Roberta emptied her drawer.' I pulled it open. Inside was an empty gin bottle and Sweetie-pie. He leered up at us.

'She's left Sweetie-pie behind,' said Dorothy, puzzled. 'Now why on earth would she do that?'

'What shall we do with him?' I asked.

'Put him in the gash bucket,' said Dorothy firmly.

'In the what?' said Ruth.

Dorothy dropped him in the wastepaper basket with a splintering crash.

I said to Ruth, 'When you've unpacked we'll show you round.'

'Aren't you working this afternoon?'

'No, we've got a make-do-and-mend.'

'Make what?'

'Free half day.'

'Oh. If you could just show me where to go for tea.'

'The Mess Deck. Past the Quarter Deck.'

'And what about laundry?'

'You can send eight items a week. Two collars count as one.' Dorothy said, 'One girl sent hers in a linen laundry bag, and it came back with the laundry bag washed and ironed and wrapped in the dirty shirt.'

Ruth digested this. 'The only other thing is,' she said, 'I've forgotten my soap. Is there anywhere I can get any?'

'You can have half mine,' Dorothy told her. 'You'll have to wait for Pay Parade. You form fours with your toes on a chalk line, and when your number is called you step forward and say, "98765 sir" and put your Pay Book down inside a white square and they put a pound note and a soap coupon down on it.'

Ruth looked deeply impressed.

'Are you both New Wrens too?' she asked.

'Good heavens no,' I said indignantly. 'We've been in two weeks.'

I thought her mouth twitched.

'Just one other thing,' she said, 'could you tell me where the heads are?'

'?'

'Yes – the lav.' She gave me a deadpan look.

Suddenly we all burst out laughing. We lay on the single bed and rocked with laughter until the tears rolled down our cheeks. When we sat up I said, 'Have some chocolate,' and Dorothy said, 'What were you doing in Civvy Street?'

Ruth said, 'Well – don't tell the others, I don't want to put them off. Actually I've been at Somerville for three years. I'm a coder here.'

I didn't know it, but Ruth was destined for a Commission as a Cypher Officer.

The door crashed open and Betty burst in. 'Look at my tiddley skirt, I just got out of the window to have a look at the new ratings coming in, and it's split right up the side.'

'This is Ruth,' I said. 'She's OK.'

'That's a good thing,' said Betty, 'because what I came to say is that Vivienne in my cabin has got her 21st on Friday and we want to do a surprise feast for her after lights out, so can we use your cabin?'

'What about food?'

'We've got that all worked out. It's Wednesday today, so tonight we'll all ring up our mothers and ask them to bake cakes tomorrow morning and put them in the post in the afternoon and we'll get the parcels first thing on Friday morning.'

And thanks to the impeccably efficient wartime Post Office, all the cakes arrived first post, carefully handled and delivered because they were marked 'Cake, fragile'.

One mother had sent a large tin of condensed milk. We dug holes in the cakes with a nail file and poured condensed milk in, and spread jam an inch thick over the tops. It was a marvellous party, conducted in whispers and torchlight. We never really got all the condensed milk off the chest of drawers. Things stuck to it afterwards.

6

Food

The weeks started to rush by. Retrospective time became punctured by significant events like The Night the Hanging Cupboard Fell. This happened to me twice later in life, once in a bedsitter and once in an hotel, but never again with quite such dramatic impact, literally and metaphorically. It was the milk bottles on top, I think, so many, ricochetting against the iron bedsteads. At first I was quite sure the sentry was firing at a party of German paratroopers just outside the window. We all shot out of bed, but couldn't at first get to the light switch because the floor was heaped with six pairs of shoes, three respirators, four large biscuit tins, a suitcase and a greatcoat. It was quite a long time, groping in the dark, before we realised what had happened.

In the ten days before a carpenter put the cupboard back, we hung our clothes round the light flex and fused all the lights. It didn't much matter – it was nearly midsummer and light enough to lie in bed chanting our signal flag lists until late in the evening.

'Go on,' I said to Dorothy, 'how do you remember flag C?'

'Black to the hoist, blue to the fly, red to the deck and yellow on high.' The flag was divided into four different triangles by two diagonal lines.

'Number three', I said.

'Oh murder. Is it white with a blue St George's cross?'

'No, that's two.'

'I shall never never remember them all. We've only done the alphabetical flags and the numbers, there are twenty-six special flags and twenty-four pendants to come, and the substitutes. And then we start on the International Code, all different. I just can't think how to begin.'

Ruth, who was lying on her bunk reading *Picture Post*, cleared her throat apologetically. 'I don't want to butt in, but if you like I could help you with methods of studying – planning and ways to learn chunks of facts and that sort of thing.'

From then on she coached us, rewarding us with her cautious,

29

pleased smile when we got it right. I had always liked learning by heart, which helped. Ruth never seemed to have to work hard at her own coding exams, but she always came top of her class.

She helped us to memorise the definitions. 'What is "at the dip"?' I would babble back, 'A signal is at the dip when it is hoisted about three quarters of the full extent of the halyards.' 'What is a series?' 'A series consists of two or more contiguous flags or pendants of any one of the following classes – alphabetical flags, special flags, numeral flags, numbered pendants, or special pendants, in any hoist which in themselves compose a separate signal.'

'Gather round,' said Chief on the Parade Ground, opening the lid of an oblong wooden box. Up popped a metal mast with tiny hooks down each side. In the box were rows of little metal flags. 'If you know the meaning of the signal write it down – if you don't, write down the names of the flags. Each couple, take a telescope. And don't take your signal cards with you and look them up!' he shouted after us, as we trailed off in pairs to the furthest corners and knelt in the grass, one focussing the telescope on the tiny metal mast in the distance, and the other getting out a notebook and pencil.

'He's slotting in the first one,' said Dorothy. 'It's that pendant with four squares, red and white. Underneath there's a flag – yellow, red, yellow stripe.'

'Interrogative,' I said, 'and D. I think I know that – it's "request permission to enter harbour".'

'Do you think we'll ever really need to know all this?' she asked.

'I don't know,' I said, rolling over on my back in the long grass with my hands behind my head and looking at the blue sky and listening to the birds. 'But isn't it absolutely heavenly? Think of sitting in an office in London typing – or rather don't.' My shirt sleeves were rolled up and my arms were getting quite sunburnt.

On Saturday afternoons we could 'go ashore on the 1300 hours liberty boat'. We lined up on the Quarter Deck to be inspected, and had a long list of rules and regulations read to us, ending with 'The Casino Dance Hall Warrington is out of bounds to all Wrens and ratings.' Whatever dire happening had resulted in this prohibition was never disclosed, but of course the Yanks were in Warrington.

Once past the White Ensign and off the Quarter Deck we hobbled as fast as our new shoes would let us up the road to the roundabout. From here you could hitch to Liverpool, Manchester, Warrington, Chester, Leigh, Newton, Lymm, and Earlstown.

Rita was the first to go out of camp in uniform. She hitched to Warrington to see an aunt who kept a grocer's shop. She was walking up the shopping street when to her horror she saw a Wren officer approaching. All the nerves in her body seemed to rush into her right arm until it felt enormous and as heavy as lead. Nearer and nearer she got, her eyes riveted on the officer's cap, until they were level. She passed by, her feet helplessly moving but her arm unable to. The officer came back and said crossly, 'Haven't you been taught to salute?'

'Oh yes, ma'am,' said Rita abjectly, 'but I wasn't quite sure.'

'Well, be sure another time,' said the officer.

Judy usually flagged down the hitches. She looked misleadingly innocent, a chubby child with strawy scarecrow hair.

We hitched to Liverpool in a lorry with a trailer, which had a chimney belching black smoke sticking up over the cab. Some sailors pulled us into the trailer when it drew up at the roundabout, but the driver got out and said, 'Put the Wrens in the front bit, it's cleaner there,' so we balanced along the iron towing bar and the driver put down a greasy tarpaulin for us to lie on at the back of the lorry. He handed us carefully down on the outskirts of Liverpool, and we got on a tram to Pierhead and carried on to New Brighton and went on a boating pool and rode the donkeys on the sands.

We hitched to Manchester, sitting in a row along the side of a very long trailer with our legs hanging over the edge. Betty took safety pins with her as she always split her skirt when hitching. She said eighteen inches off the ground was the limit for her to hitch. As we chugged through the suburbs we waved and blew kisses to everyone, and they waved and blew kisses back. In Manchester we went to the Sadlers Wells Ballet which was on tour, with Fonteyn and Helpmann in *Hamlet,* and Constant Lambert doing the commentary in *Wedding Bouquet.*

We hitched to Warrington in a closed-in cattle lorry. It was pitch dark, the floor was covered in straw and the walls were slimy and sticky. When the driver banged down the metal rod that locked the back doors, we were packed in so tight with sailors that we couldn't move our arms. When we went round corners the whole solid mass of us swayed shrieking from side to side. We sucked treacle toffees to drown the cattle smell. We emerged blinking at Warrington, our uniforms smeary with fat.

We hitched to Leigh in a huge lorry full of aeroplane frames, squeezed into the space between the frames and the cab. We hitched to Chester, in a lorry full of red paint, with disastrous effect on our uniforms.

Wherever we hitched, it was with one purpose – food. In spite of the frequent parcels with which our devoted families supplemented the rather emasculated meals in camp, we were always starving. Perhaps it was giving up a sedentary life for an open air one, or the amount of mental and physical energy we were using up, or the insecurity of being away from home and never knowing if the next meal would be edible, but we could eat anything, any time, anywhere. We couldn't have been anywhere better than Lancashire, which seemed stuffed with ample, beaming women saying, 'Have some more, loov, I've got a son down south, hope someone's feeding him.'

Like the little birds we were named after, we found it hard work to maintain our body temperature from day to day. If not quite able to eat our own weight daily, on Saturdays we chirruped our way from Earlstown Church Canteen (baked beans on toast, peas, chips, toast, jam, cake, tea, 6½d) to the White Swan (baked beans on toast, and toast and jam and tea and damsons and custard, 1s) to the WVS canteen (salad, fruit cake, tea, 4d) to the YMCA canteen (buttered toast, chips, currant buns, tea, chocolate biscuits, peppermints, shortbread, cake, 1s).

Between Manchester and Lowton St Mary's you changed at Irlam, with ten minutes to spare. There was just time to run to the fish and chip shop and back. 'How much can we have?' 'As mooch as you like loov,' they said. We saw tomatoes in a shop – the first for years. 'Are they for *sale?*' we timidly asked. 'Do up a pound bag of tomatoes for each of the Wrens,' the man said to his assistant.

We waited at a bus stop when we got off the hitch in Liverpool. 'Come on now, Navy on first,' said the conductor, 'they're all far from home,' and the shoppers stood back beaming and said,

'That's reet.' It seemed a wonderful county, with wonderful, generous, cheerful people. On inoculation and vaccination day nearly everybody fainted in Sick Bay, and then went to bed with a temperature. Only two of us had certificates showing that we had Been Done, so we were allowed out of camp. We hitched to Leigh with shopping commissions from everybody else, and finished up in a cafe where the woman said, 'Will meat pie and fish pie and potatoes and bread and butter and tea and ginger cake be enough for a shilling loovs?'

In the Forces canteen at New Brighton, at 1500, we had fish cakes, potatoes, bread and butter, coffee, apple tart, and blancmange for 1s 2d. We went back to Liverpool and had corned beef and rice pudding for 6d. Then on to Warrington for pease pudding and toast at the YMCA. Then on to Lowton Church Canteen for pork pies and coffee, and back to camp for chocolate cake and fizzy lemonade.

At the Dingle Café at Lymm we sat out on a lawn with chickens pecking round us and had cold meat, tomatoes, cucumber, bread and butter, a pot of apricot jam, scones, cakes and tea for 2s. I was still hungry.

On the hitches back, when everyone was in a mellow mood, the sailors sang in the backs of the lorries.

Now this is number one, and the fun has just begun,
Roll me over, lay me down, and do it again,
Roll me over, in the clover,
Roll me over, lay me down, and do it again.

They sang, and we listened, because we never could get hold of all the words. If we thought we knew a verse, they would say, 'Ah, but that's the expurgated version.' If we did get the words right, we weren't sure that we understood what they meant.

It was the same with the tattooed lady.

And all around her hips, are rows of battleships,
And over her kidney is a birds-eye view of Sydney ...

Betty said, 'Somehow I'll *make* Chief tell me the real Navy version.'

7

The First Boat

'Right!' said Chief. 'So you can read naval flags. Now you're going to hoist them. First I'll teach you to break colours. Jackets off, sleeves rolled up, two teams – red and blue, one standing by each flag locker under the mast. The first one who lets a halyard go has to climb the mast after it.'

We looked up. The mast was very high, about eight times our height. The flag lockers were almost our height, grey square steel boxes on end, with ninety pigeon-holes in each for the flags.

When we pulled them out, the flags were much bigger than we had imagined, as big as bedspreads. We tripped over them and wound them round our feet. Each flag had a large brass clip, like an almost closed C, at the top corner, and a bit of halyard with another clip on the end at the bottom corner. The clip slotted into the one on the next flag. If you didn't attach the top flag to the halyard, which came from the masthead or the yardarm, you were in trouble – when you hoisted the signal the string of flags remained in a sad pile at your feet like dirty washing and the top clip went waving up out of reach. Sometimes you had to include a tackline – a long stretch of halyard with a clip each end – which separated two flag signals.

When you pulled down flag signals, you had to unclip them, and stow them in their correct pigeon-holes, parcelled up to come out easily, with the two brass clips hanging over the edge of the pigeon-hole.

'Wait for the command,' shouted Chief, 'are you ready?'

We stood poised, our hands hovering over the rows of neatly parcelled flags in the locker.

'This is the signal – "My message, time of origin 1450, is cancelled." Bend on!'

The Negative Flag, and numeral flags one four five zero. We bumped into each other, reaching across the locker, all thumbs with clips. 'Bent on, Chief.'

'HOIST!' roared Chief.

We hauled, and up went the flags, rather slow and jerky. We dared to look up. Surprisingly, they were up the right way and in the right order, one line reaching the top just before the other. Five marks to the red team.

We swelled with pride. How marvellous the flags looked, fluttering in the summer breeze against the blue sky. Almost as if we were on a real ship.

Chief said, 'You've got to spend four months inland, but they want you to feel part of the Navy so they've arranged a trip next Saturday afternoon to Liverpool and you'll be shown over a minesweeper.

At last I would be Getting on a Boat! I was speechless with excitement, until I talked to Judy. 'I'm not going on any rotten old minesweeper,' she said. 'Let the rest of them go if they want to. One of the sailors told me that if you go to Liverpool Docks and show your Pay Book they'll let you on the docks and then you can get on anything.'

Celia and Betty and Judy and I did this. It was like magic. We got off the overhead railway at the docks, and when we showed our Pay Books the sentry waved us in. We picked our way round cranes and bollards, our eyes round with wonder at the sheer enormousness of it all, the miles of grey shapes moored alongside.

We walked along a quay beside a grey iron wall which towered into the sky and stretched behind and in front of us as far as we could see. A fragile gang plank wavered up into infinity. The sailor at the bottom end shouted, 'Coming aboard, girls?' He seemed about our age.

We looked at each other. This was it. Up we went.

We gazed round on a deck which seemed bigger than ten football pitches. 'What is it?' said Judy.

The sailor said, 'She's the *Gambia*. A Fiji Class cruiser.'

First go, and we'd got on one of the biggest things afloat!

A marine said, 'I'll show you round.'

We clanged and clanked up and down ladders, from deck to deck, we saw the radar room and the W/T room and the engine room. The marines grinned as they passed us. Everything echoed – miles and miles of long grey echoing passages; stepping over watertight doors, past portholes. It wasn't a ship, it was a city.

Judy was pink in the face with an idea, her shorn spikes of

yellow hair sticking out round her cap. She hissed, 'I'm going to spend a penny in the Captain's bathroom!'

We whispered back, shocked, 'You can't!'

Judy said to the marine, 'Can we see the Captain's quarters?'

He said, 'You can see the lot – the officers are all ashore.'

Judy came beaming out of the Captain's bathroom. 'It's all blue tiles,' she whispered.

The marine said, 'The lads are all having tea in the Mess now, come and join us.'

On the Mess Deck there were miles of long scrubbed tables bolted down, and long benches. Marines were cramming doorsteps of bread into their mouths. There were two pound blocks of butter, five pound tins of plum jam, tin mugs of indigo tea topped up with condensed milk and brown sugar until it was solid.

We swopped addresses; we said, 'Write to us, we'll write to you.' We came back to camp in a daze of glory. We were part of the war, part of the Navy.

Marianne said, 'You ought to have come, it was terrific, we went to Liverpool and got on a minesweeper.'

Betty said, '*We* went to Liverpool and got on a cruiser!'

Half way through the course we went on leave. Before that we took our Badge Test, in morse, semaphore, flag signals, coding and message procedure. Chief had given up most of his weekends and evenings to coaching us, and stayed in camp all the weekend after the Test in case the results came out early. We kept meeting him, looking more and more haggard. There were rumours that if the results were bad he would be moved. He was so young and the classes were so hilarious that the officers didn't believe we had really learnt anything.

On Monday morning Dracula came in, looking embittered as usual, and told us that we had all passed, and that it was the first time since the camp opened that a whole class had achieved this. We were delirious with excitement.

Chief read out the marks, and said to Dracula, pointing at me, 'That one got 100% for morse.' Dracula said, 'That's good – demmed good.' It was the best moment of my life.

Chief handed out our badges – crossed flags – which we button-holed on to our right jacket sleeves. We illegally embroidered V/S underneath them. None of us had dared tell our families about the badges, in case we didn't get them.

Bursting with pride, we got on the train at Lowton St Mary's to go home, our cases full of bellbottoms and skirts for our mothers to alter.

We were half way to being Real Wrens.

8

The Prototype

'What the devil,' said Old Snoopy, bursting into the lecture room, 'what the devil is all this noise about, Chief?'

Chief pulled his face straight. 'It's the International Signals Code, sir.'

Judy mopped her streaming eyes and laid her head weakly on her desk. 'It's so funny,' she sobbed, 'so funny.'

'Well, carry on Chief,' said Snoopy blandly, leaning against the blackboard.

Chief gave him a despairing look. 'As I said, the meaning of the first group of flags hoisted, was "Is there room for me in your berth?"'

We sat in silence, our eyes on our desks, our lips twitching.

The next one was, "Keep close to me in the dark."'

We dared to shoot a glance at Old Snoopy. His saturnine face was slightly pink.

'After that, I gave you "The buoy you are approaching is not in a proper position."'

Judy gave a snuffling snort.

'Next one, "My bottom is damaged in two places."'

There was a roar of laughter.

'"The buoy to which you are attached is not to be depended on." I'm sorry sir,' said Chief through the pandemonium. 'I've got to teach them. If you were a young lady, could you keep a straight face?'

We hoisted the International flags, we learnt what to look up in which Confidential Books, we were introduced to BR619, the Pendant List, which would be our bible, the FSB (Fleet Signals Book) and the AVSB (Auxiliary Vessels Signals Book), we learnt that in morse you always flashed Ireland (R) and Iceland (C) in case someone read one dash too many and sent the convoy to the wrong place. We learnt about asdics and radiolocation, which were the newest thing. We learnt the Code Word Appendix, and the Distinguishing Signals, and the Alarm Signal Table, and the

Sector System for Aircraft, and anchorage and harbour signals, and catapulting and alighting signals for aircraft carriers, and message prosigns, and the abbreviated plain language table. We learnt to flash U for you, and R for are, and how to say 'wait' and 'repeat' and 'delete'. We spent hours and hours every day on the parade ground, reading morse, until it came out of our ears and we saw dots and dashes all night.

'Next you must read in words,' Chief said. 'Spread out!' I riveted my eyes to his lamp, not daring to blink. Dorothy's pencil was poised in awful anxiety over the buff 'flashing exercise' form, as instead of getting a letter at a time from me she had to wait until I had strung together a word in my mind to dictate to her. The pauses between words were so short that if you missed one dot you could get a whole sentence wrong.

'U – that's you – R – that's are – to – proceed – to – a – position – two – seven – one – degrees – one – point – five – miles – devils point – join – convoy – proceeding – eastward – full stop.'

I could do it. I had the knack. It was better than talking. It was my language from now on. We could all do it, except Vivienne. She was so attractive she didn't have to bother. The day of the flashing exam, when Chief shouted 'Spread out!' she took the place nearest to him and just as he started on the test message she tottered towards him and fell in a dead faint at his feet. With great gallantry he carefully put the lamp down, gathered her up, and carried her into the Assembly Hall.

She failed her exam, but 'It was worth it,' she said, with a glint in her eye.

We went to a Yank dance in Warrington. Once in the arms of a real live Yank, you forgot the prohibitions and disapprovals and succumbed to the magic. They could dance properly, even a slow foxtrot.

You are the promised breath of springtime
That makes the lonely winter seem long
You are – the breathless hush of evening
That trembles on the brink of a lovely song –

Your hand was on that smooth, pale, beautiful cloth, your eye was level with the US shoulder flash.

You are the angel glow, that lights a star,
The dearest things I know, are what you are

They had proper shoes, not hobnail boots, and they never trod on your feet.

'Relax, honey,' murmured my Yank, just like James Stewart.

Some day, my happy arms will hold you,
And some day, I'll know that moment divine,
When all the things you are, are mine ...

At the drop of a hat I would have gone on to the Casino Dance Hall, Warrington. With very little persuasion I'd have gone for a GI Bride. But after an experienced kiss and a 'goodnight, honey' he was gone, and the Cinderellas were shepherded back to camp.

One evening, Zara said, 'No wonder you can't get boy friends, you all look so plain. I have all these cosmetics I brought from Brazil, I shall make you up.'

Eight of us squashed into her cabin. She worked grimly at our weather-beaten faces. She had brought masses of everything. She stuck on false eyelashes and plastered us with pancake and smeared on navy blue eye-shadow and outlined cupids bows in vermilion and scooped our hair up on top of our heads. We looked fantastic – even a Yank would have been frightened off. There was nowhere to go so we had to take it all off again.

We sat the final exam, with practical tests in semaphore, ten-inch, and Aldis, and papers in V/S procedure, coding practice, and V/S general. When the results came out Chief was so relieved he hired a taxi and took eight of us out to dinner in Manchester. We had saved his reputation.

A form came round on which we could enter our first choice for a draft. We all put Portsmouth, except Betty, the realist.

'Of course I want to go to Portsmouth,' she explained, 'but the last few classes have all gone to Scotland, and I don't want to go there. I'm going to Ireland.'

I said, 'Ireland? What on earth do you want to go there for?'

'Better than Scotland – you'll see,' she said. 'Why don't you come too – it'll be such *fun.*'

But my luck had held so far, and I had a naive faith that if you

40

really wanted something and turned a deaf ear to all the people who said it was impossible, you might get it.

We all went to Scotland, except Betty who went to Larne. But before we knew where we were to go, we went on leave. For the last time we trooped out of camp and dragged our cases down to the platform at Lowton St Mary's.

Having been melted down, we had come out of the mould. Outwardly, we looked much more alike than when we had arrived, and as looking alike appears to be the main object of the young, this gave us great satisfaction. We also had the advantage of achieving this object without facing the disapproval of our elders, which left our rebellious energy free to be expressed in other ways. We had all filled out on the starchy food, we were brown and healthy, and our uniforms more or less fitted. Our voices were much, much louder.

We had acquired a sort of brashness which might pass for confidence in social life. In work we didn't need it – we were the tops and we knew it. It was a superb training, and equipped us to compete with signalmen anywhere under any conditions. If they had told us we were going straight to the bridge of the *Warspite*, or to be dropped over Hamburg to start a signal station there, we would have known we could do it better than anyone else.

Ganavan.

II

Bonnie Oban Bay

1

Oban

While I was on leave, my draft came through. 'Report to your nearest RTO,' it said, 'for travel instructions.' I went to the one in Trafalgar Square. 'I've got to get to Oban,' I said. "Olborn?" the man said. 'Easy as pie dear, on the Piccadilly Line from Leicester Square.'

Pauline, Dorothy, Sue and I from *Cabbala* met at Euston at 1930 one evening in October. Our hearts were at the bottom of our clumping black lace-up shoes. We couldn't think of any mitigating aspect of a draft to Oban. We all wanted to go to Portsmouth, where the war at sea was being fought, not to mention the war of the sexes.

We had never travelled all night before. By making faces at other prospective travellers we managed to start the journey with a carriage to ourselves.

Half an hour later the train stopped at Bletchley and eight Scottish Royal Engineers got in, in a welter of greatcoats and kitbags and respirators. They were seasoned night travellers, and once the train started again and we had shared the sandwiches and cake our mums had fondly packed up for us they drew down the blinds, took out the light bulbs, and we all took off our collars and ties and settled down in a sweaty sprawl of serge. There were no wandering hands, no winks and innuendoes. The two priorities for Other Ranks of all the Services were food and sleep, with sex a bad third. We all sank into a stupor.

At 0300 I was roused by a voice of hollow doom intoning 'Carlisle, this is Carlisle,' and ever after those syllables have echoed in my brain as an expression of ultimate despair, far more potent than the Raven's 'Nevermore'. It was always dark and always raining at Carlisle.

It was still dark when we had to change at Stirling. There should have been a two hour wait, there usually was at Stirling, on a pitch dark platform in drenching rain, but that first time our train was two hours late so we only just caught the Oban train. As the dawn came up we puffed on through the Highlands, up and down the glens, round and about the lochs. The sky was dark grey and a solid curtain of rain fell. Sue had been standing in the corridor ever since Stirling, snivelling quietly, her tears running down inside the window as fast as the rain outside. Suddenly she raised an arm and, pointing a shaking finger at the barely visible hillside, wailed, 'Look, oh look! Highland Cattle! Oh, oh I want to go home! Highland Cattle!' and she burst into renewed sobs.

At midday we chugged into Oban. Sue was billeted near the Pier, with Dorothy. There was a transport waiting to take Pauline and me to our quarters. We crawled over the tailboard and sat shivering and yawning under the dripping canvas top. My case was in the open, and I could see my new rug, a rather smart pale blue and mauve Shetland affair strapped to the outsid, with the rain soaking into it until the colours merged to an overall dark grey.

The transport took us out along the seashore to the north, past a line of houses so gaunt, so colourless, so dour, so unimaginative, that they appeared merely an extension of the seeping sheets of rain. It stopped outside a grey granite pile with lowering gables. This was Raasay Lodge (we called it Rassy, which infuriated the purists on both sides of the border). I thought it looked a place of gothic doom, of sepulchral cold, of desolation of spirit. We splashed our way in and found ourselves in a very large dark room with walls and ceiling entirely panelled in pitchpine, and a scored bare board floor.

The room contained six hard chairs and a horsehair sofa, a very old upright piano, a pitted dart board, a black marble windowseat, a bucket of coal, a rickety card table with a jigsaw puzzle on it, a jam jar with six chrysanthemums, and sundry war maps pinned up round the pitchpine. Blackout curtains hung beside the sash windows. The decor of Raasay Lodge was a prime example of making the absolute and unspeakable worst of a climate and situation which seemed designed by nature to create the maximum amount of misery.

While we clanked about waiting for someone to tell us what to do, I glanced at the Notice Board. In pride of place was a large notice signed by the Naval Officer in Charge of the Base informing all Wrens that no request for a draft from Oban, even on compassionate or health grounds, could be considered until the rating concerned had served there for at least two years. I thought, but I shall be middle-aged by then. Or dead.

The Duty Orderly clumped over the echoing boards. 'Ye'll no be sleeping here,' she said. 'Ye'll be up the glen. I'll tek ye.' She began to pull on wellingtons and oilskins. Up the glen indeed, I thought. A bothy by a burn I don't doubt. She looked pityingly at our issue raincoats, which had kept out the Lancashire rain so satisfactorily. 'Ye'll need some clothing when the autumn comes,' she said.

As we squelched behind her out of the gate we passed a gnarled figure doing something incomprehensible to the gravel with a fierce looking metal prong. 'Yon's Auld Hamish,' the Orderly said. 'He was the auld leddy's gardener.'

Up the road we followed her. The 'glen' turned out to be Glen Campa, ever after known as Glen Dampa.

Raasay Lodge, where the Mess, the Wren Officers, and most of the Wrens were accommodated, was rumoured to have been a private house before the war, owned by an old lady in her nineties who lived there with an equally ancient and eccentric retainer. Glen Campa could never have been anything but a cheeseparing sort of mid-Victorian boarding house at the wrong end of town. It was used to provide overflow accommodation for the Wrens. Our cabin had bare floorboards, mauve and green wallpaper peeling off in stained patches, a sash window with a broken cord, and a small blackened grate of the kind now lovingly restored by connoisseurs with central heating. Later, I spent all one Saturday afternoon trying to light a fire in it. Eventually, after holding newspaper over it until I was smoke-dried, I came to the conclusion that the fireplace was purely decorative. Or perhaps there were bagpipes stuffed up the chimney.

The cabin was furnished with a single iron bed, a double bunk, a small battered chest with three drawers that didn't open, and a large leaning wardrobe that didn't shut, with piles of cardboard boxes on top. The room was in a perpetual Celtic twilight, as, for some unfathomable reason, there were early Victorian venetian blinds at the north window, which would not stay up. The cold and the damp were quite palpable, almost visible.

There was no heating at all in the house, no gas or coal or oil,

47

and one cold water tap in the bathroom. The mice were so hungry they used to eat the soap. When we cycled off watch at 2300 in December in a deluge, we used to strip off our clothes on the landing and hang them over the banister to drip all night into the tiled hall below, and then drag them on again in the morning. When we came off watch at 0800 we had to go to Raasay Lodge for breakfast, then back to Glen Campa for our towels and soap, then back to Raasay Lodge for a bath, then dress and go back to Glen Campa and undress and get into bed.

But that first afternoon the trials of a watchkeeper were mercifully hidden from me. I had arrived in Bonnie Oban Bay, I was a real Wren in my first Base, helping to win the war, to Free a Man to Join the Fleet.

In the years after the war I was often to hear friends describe idyllic holidays in Oban, the Pearl of the Hebrides; the Western Highlands and Islands, car trips, caravan trips, boat trips, hoots in the heather, stags in the glen, sunsets in the Trossachs. I always had to maintain a stunned silence to conceal my utter inability to believe that they were describing the same place. Can those gaunt, grim, perishingly cold stone edifices actually be occupied by summer visitors? Perhaps they have painted the bleak facades in candy colours with striped sunblinds, like the Gorgon's head in drag. But what could they do about the rain?

For the next eighteen months I was never to go in a car; there were two long winters of blackout; you couldn't get to any of the islands (but we did); to go in the train as far as Loch Awe was out of bounds (but we did); you were not allowed on a boat (but that's another story).

2

Ganavan

It stopped raining in the night. Next day five Wren signallers walked the mile north out of town to Ganavan War Signal Station. We were to be introduced by the Base Signalman, Dave, to the naval ratings whose shore jobs we were taking over to enable them to go to sea. Pauline and I walked out from Glen Campa; Carol, Rosemary and Joan from Raasay Lodge. Carol grinned and said 'Hallo there!' Rosemary said 'Hallo toots,' and Joan, who, even muffled up in naval serge, could not help looking elegant, gave us a cool smile. There was something about the way Joan turned her head, about her large, expressive eyes, which indicated to me that she had studied dancing.

We passed Dunollie Point, a largish hillock crowned by the remains of the keep of Dunollie Castle, round the edge of the bay, past the foot of a small cliff, and up the further side of it to where the Signal Station perched on top. It was the highest point for miles, with breathtaking views. Eastwards, inland, we could see the highest mountain, Ben Cruachan. South the road wound back to Oban, the way we had come, the keep of Dunollie poking out of the trees. North along the coast was Ganavan Bay proper, the seaplane base. West was our bit of sea, enclosed by land – Kerrera Island on the left, Lismore Island on the right, Mull in front – with the Sound of Mull going round to the right of Mull and the Firth of Lorne going round to the left. In front was Maiden Island – as big as a big back garden.

From the Signal Station little cinder paths meandered down, petering out after varying lengths depending on how far the signallers could be bothered to carry the ash bucket.

The Signal Station was an oblong building on two floors. An outside lav and a coal hole stuck out at the back. Next to them was a door into the ground floor, where there was a living room and a small cabin with a double bunk. The blankets on the double bunk were dark grey and curiously stained and proved to be alive with fleas which we never succeeded in eliminating. Next to the cabin was a tiny galley with a sink and cold water tap, where we were to spend hours making jam and marmalade and winding old unravelled knitting wool round jam jars of boiling water to take out the kinks – it never really worked. There was a wooden ladder up to the signal room, which occupied all the first floor and had a railed balcony round three sides. The ten-inch lamp was on the balcony.

An outside ladder led up separately to the balcony, and was the normal way in, and another ladder led up to the flat roof on which we were privileged to stand in the snow doing semaphore when all the lamps failed. There was a high mast outside for the White Ensign and the gale cone (a large unwieldy object of sopping grey canvas which, when hoisted, must have been invisible 100 yards off shore). A metal flag locker leaned lopsidedly against the back door, and a waterlogged wooden chest on the other side was reputed to contain rockets and flares, which mercifully we were never required to use as we hadn't the faintest idea how to fire them.

The signal room had a hatch cover over the square hole where the ladder came up. In time we became adept at hauling ourselves up and down the ladder one-handed, with a kettle of boiling water, a bucket of coal, an Aldis battery, a cup of tea, or a toasted sandwich in the other hand. This peg-handed motion up and down the wooden rungs, the free hand flailing rhythmically round the next rung, by day and by night, produced a sound which became utterly evocative of Ganavan. Sometimes we missed our grip, and fell dramatically to the concrete floor below, with broken china and boiling water descending on our heads.

The signal room had windows round three sides. One on the Lismore side, over the door, and one on the side facing the sea, had upper fanlights which pushed open and up, to take the big telescope which swung out on a swivel. We had to stand on an Aldis box to see out of it. When not used for identifying ships, the big telescope could be tilted down to pick out necking couples round the bay in summer. There was a stool, and an upright chair, and two telephones, one with its flex coming out of a little box with a handle.

Against the back wall stood the stove, an iron cylinder with a let-down flap at the top to put lumps of coal in, and an oblong flap at the bottom to rake the ash out. When the wind was from the east it smoked from every crack and aperture and we had to sit outside on the balcony, rain and dark notwithstanding. After a few weeks our bellbottoms had a circular burn mark round each thigh where we had leaned over the stove and scorched them on the top rim.

On this first day the very sight of this unbeautiful object struck joy into our hearts – a stove meant that we could dry our sodden clothing, which was lying in pools of water on the linoleum bedroom floor at Glen Campa, and wash our hair, and boil a kettle. The refinements like making marmalade and dyeing old knitting wool occurred to us later.

There were framed charts and illustrated flag signals on the back wall, and an upended orange box containing a frayed pair of plimsolls and a chipped teapot. A small square of the shelf under the main window was partitioned off and had a shaded bulb over it. Crouched there on a stool was a sailor, hunched over the Log Book. I peered over his shoulder. For several days the only entry was '0730 Dunollie off. 1930 Dunollie on.' Dave explained that there was a light on the point of rock below Dunollie Castle to stop ships going aground there on entering and leaving harbour, and it was wired to the Signal Station and had to be switched on at dusk and off at dawn. Sometimes we forgot, and the next ship in or out would flash us up and say, 'You've forgotten the light, love.' It didn't really seem to matter to them if it was alight or not – at least, they never hit the rocks when it was off.

Dave handed us handleless cups of tea. There were smuts floating on top. We could imagine there always would be. There was a patina of coal dust and ash over everything, though a sketchy attempt had been made to sweep the floor with a stiff broom, leaving parallel score marks in the ash going towards the open hatch.

For us it was an historic moment, if we had realised it. In our eighteen months at Oban we would never all be together again. We gathered round and stared at Fred, the signal rating, awed at the gigantic responsibility we were taking on.

Dave said, 'Well, here you all are – freeing a man for the fleet at last. Terrific.' There was something a bit snide in the way he said it. Carol plucked up courage to say to Fred's back, 'When are you joining your ship, then?' Fred didn't turn round, he crouched lower over the Log and muttered, 'Not to sea – going to Lismore.'

'Lismore?' we said incredulously. We had heard already that there was nothing on Lismore except a few sheep and some seagulls, and surely nothing you could signal to from there except Ganavan.

'Yes,' said Dave, 'the Ganavan contingent of the Royal Navy are moving to Lismore tomorrow to further the war effort.'

The back of Fred's neck was red. We got the impression he wasn't pleased.

3

The Loops

Next morning Carol and Rosemary reported at 0800 to take over our first watch officially from Fred and Len. Joan and I relieved them at 1300. We thought what a beautiful romantic walk it was, through the autumn sunshine, better than sitting at a typewriter in London. Past Dunollie Castle on the right we went, along the shore of the little bay with a stupendous view of sea and mountains opening up on our left through a kaleidoscope of shimmering russety leaves, round the headland with its cliff face on the right, over the barbed wire fence, and then a stiff climb up the far side.

There were blankets hanging over the balcony railings. In the bright sunlight they looked very grey. Carol and Rosemary had their sleeves rolled up. 'We've been cleaning,' they said, 'it's filthy. Only one signal. There doesn't seem to be any more coal – just the bucket Fred left. Best of luck,' and they were off down the hill.

'There's a hole in the kettle,' Joan said, 'and it's awfully rusty. I wonder if Fred took the good kettle?'

'*What* did Dave say about that little 'phone with the handle on the box?' I said.

'I couldn't understand,' said Joan. 'I hoped you had. Something to do with loops.' At that minute it rang huskily.

Joan snatched it up and said in a quavering voice, 'WSS.' I could hear a male voice the other end say, 'Little Ganavan – Bert here – our DO is on the way up to check your CBs.' The line went dead.

We looked at each other thoughtfully, registering DO as Duty Officer and CBs as Confidential Books. But where were they, and why did he want to check them, and what had Dave said Little Ganavan was? Anyway, the place looked fairly clean. We rolled our shirtsleeves down and put our jackets on to be on the safe side.

Ten minutes later a rather elderly Sub-Lieutenant RNVR (thirty at least) with a propitiating expression came panting up the steps. 'It's OK,' he said, 'they're in that little grey tin box on the wall, and the key is under the telephone. Did Dave tell you I have to come and check them once a week?'

'No – oh, yes,' Joan said. It was probably politic not to let Dave down. We stood respectfully while he checked the signal and code lists.

'Dave explained about the loops, did he?' he said. 'Oh yes,' I said. 'Good, good,' he said. 'Well, remember we're not far away, if you ever want a hand.'

'Thank you,' we chorused, as he executed a deft descent of the outside ladder, missing several steps (a skill which we made a mental note to acquire as soon as possible). 'Don't forget the Ensign,' he shouted up, 'and the gale cone.'

At that moment the husky 'phone rang again. He rapidly reversed his ladder drill, coming up three at a time, and picked up the 'phone.

'WSS.'

'Little Ganavan, sir,' said a male voice. 'Crossing on one.'

He shot a practised eye over the expanse of sea. I indicated a telescope but he waved it away and snapped back, 'Fishing boat, *Maid of Mull*, outward.'

He flashed us a dazzling smile, said rather apologetically, 'She always goes out about this time,' and was away, galloping down the side of the cliff like an antelope.

It seemed odd to us that at *Cabbala*, where it didn't really matter, everyone had gone to such trouble to explain everything. Here, where it patently did matter, nobody thought any explanations necessary. We tried to piece it together.

'There are two loops,' said Joan, 'one stretching across the Firth of Lorne and one across the Sound of Mull, under the sea.'

'And every time a boat crosses one of them it gives off a bleep.'

'Where?'

'In Little Ganavan!'

'But where *is* Little Ganavan?'

'Could it be all that barbed wire and notices saying no admittance, RN property, at the bottom of the cliff? That's the only thing that's quite near.'

'You can't see any buildings. They must be right on the beach.'

'Then they sit there watching a radar screen – have you ever seen a radar screen?'

'Yes – a little round window in the dark – there was one on the battleship we got on in Liverpool docks. It's awfully new – the latest thing. Sort of green and blurry, with a wiggly line going across the middle. When it sees anything, the line jumps up and down.'

'So when it does that, they 'phone us up and say "crossing on one" or "crossing on two" and we look at the sea and tell them what ship it is.'

'Supposing we don't know.'

'We flash it up, you clot, and get its name.'

'How do we see it at night?'

'I suppose it'll have some lights.'

'And supposing we can't see anything?'

'Then we tell them, and it must be a submarine.'

We looked at each other with widening eyes, visualising a sleek sinister shape gliding into Bonnie Oban Bay to blow it to bits, or to land Conrad Veidt in dark glasses at Dunollie Point to mastermind a plot to assassinate Churchill. It would all be our fault.

I looked again at the sea. 'I don't know how he could see that fishing boat,' I muttered. 'And we've got to know whether it's naval and we give it the code of the day challenge, or international and we give it the unknown ship call.'

This was the least of our worries in point of fact. Quite small objects like hunks of driftwood gave out bleeps. Small non-naval vessels were bloody-minded about giving their identity or even acknowledging their existence. At night you were lucky if they showed a kiddies' night-light at the masthead. You were in clover if in addition you could pick out a port and starboard, thus indicating whether the vessel was going out or coming in, and its approximate size.

One pitch black night I gave the challenge to a barely moving candle creeping along by Maiden Island, which returned a long and totally incomprehensible series of dots and dashes. I had a pretty good idea it was a launch called the *Caledonia*, and the next day when I met the skipper in town I said, 'What the hell were you playing at with your morse last night?' He replied in an injured tone, 'My morse is vairry guid – I was spelling out "Caledonia sterrn and wild".'

We did eventually get the hang of the system, which was to

watch the sea and get our word in first – wind the handle and hope it made them jump at Little Ganavan over their tea and fags, and say smartly, 'MacBrayne's steamer, crossing two in five minutes.'

It always seemed to me an extremely cumbersome and costly way of keeping the Germans out, particularly as it also involved the two anti-submarine trawlers, the *Southern Wave* and the *Southern Star*, which pottered back and forth over the same patch of sea on sweeps. Their high-rearing bows, backward tilting funnels, and rather bright camouflage became as familiar as the postman and the milkman to a suburban housewife. Soon we could tell them on a dark night by the shape of the triangle made by the masthead, port and starboard lights.

When the moon made a beautifully clear path over the sea, I used to look out and imagine the two loops, like huge skeins of knitting wool, curled across the ocean bed with fishes nibbling at them.

'How marvellous it would be,' I said to Joan, 'to get actually *on* a boat.'

4

Getting on a Boat (Illegal)

At the opposite end of Oban from Ganavan, the road went on past the pier and southwards along the coast. The mountains rose up inland on the left, and on the right, across a quarter of a mile of the Sound of Kerrera, was Kerrera Island. Dorothy and I walked glumly along there one afternoon soon after we got to Oban, complaining spasmodically to each other about being so far away from the war, and the food, and the lack of men, and the cold and damp.

As the road left Oban behind our spirits rose, and as if to encourage us the sun came out, the sky turned brilliant blue and cloudless, and the sea was a glittering sheet of silver. It was our first experience of this chameleon quality of the Highlands and we were dazzled into speechlessness and walked along in a daze. As it was Sunday we had come on from Church Parade in clean white shirts, and skirts and black silk stockings.

After about an hour we came to Gallanach Bay. Drawn up on the beach beside the road was a tiny dinghy glistening with new varnish, and standing despondently beside it were three quite beautiful RNVR Sub-Lieutenants in exquisite brand-new uniforms. As we walked rather sheepishly by, one of them said tentatively, 'Would you like a sail?'

As the five of us stepped perilously into the dinghy, the sea came almost up to the rowlocks. We didn't care – the sun was warm, the air still, and the sea like glass. They began to row rather splashily out into Kerrera Sound. The water was so clear you could see the seaweed a long way down. We trailed our fingers over the side and smiled dreamily to each other.

'Our ship only anchored here last night,' said one. 'We're at Tobermory, on Mull, the working-up base for convoy escorts. I'm John, by the way, and this is Michael, and Peter.' 'We pinched the dinghy to get ashore,' said Peter, 'to see if there's a town anywhere, but we can't find anything but mountains.'

I said, 'There's Oban – do you want us to tell you the way there?'

Michael said, 'Actually, I think you'd better not because we shall get a fearful rocket if we're seen with you – we're forbidden to take Wrens on boats.'

Dorothy beamed. 'And we're forbidden to go on boats. The First Lieutenant says so.'

John said, 'There's a little island over there, with a couple of goats on it. How about making for that? There can't be a Jimmy the One there, unless he's been turned into a goat.'

It was further than it looked, and we were busy talking and didn't look up until suddenly splashes of rain fell on us and we realised that the sky had turned black and a typical Oban rainstorm was about to descend. John and Peter had left their beautiful jackets on the shore and were rowing in their shirtsleeves. None of us had a raincoat. They pulled hard for the island. Even to my impressionable eyes their rowing looked a trifle inept.

The island was bare and stony. John said, perhaps there was a cave. The water near the shore was thick with seaweed and very rocky, but we scrambled out up to the ankles in water and pulled the dinghy up by its painter. It was pelting down by then and a howling gale had arisen. We huddled behind the largest rock we could find. Michael took his jacket off and folded it inside out to protect it. We were soon wet through, and I looked at Dorothy's hair hanging straight and dripping round her hat and knew mine was the same.

Michael and Peter made a dash back to the beach to try and prop the dinghy up as a shelter, and we squelched after them. When we came round the rocks, Peter was standing guiltily in torrential rain with half an oar in each hand – he had pulled the dinghy on top of it and snapped it. The other two looked helplessly at him and then both started to laugh. 'We'll never make it at Tobermory,' said John.

They propped the dinghy on its side on the two halves of oar and we all sat underneath it on the other oar with our knees up. It kept the worst of the rain off. Even sitting there in the slanting rain, the three of them still looked so chubby and fair and pink that I couldn't decide if I was in *Peter Pan* or *Mary Rose*.

Michael laboriously untwisted the painter and tried to splice the oar, but he didn't seem much good at it. It began to get quite choppy, and we could see a strong current setting in, away from the shore. Dorothy reminded me that it was 1600 and she was on duty at 1800 at the Pier Signal Station. I reminded her that I was on duty at 1800 at Ganavan. It didn't seem to matter very much – we were now too wet to care.

After a long time the sky got even blacker and the rain even heavier, and we were all so cold and wet we thought we might as well move on as sit there. John said, 'If we carried the dinghy over the island we'd be that much nearer the land and wouldn't have so far to row.' So we did that, skidding over the tufts of squelching grass. The two goats watched us pityingly, their sodden plus-fours clinging round their knees. When we came over the top and down the other side we saw what looked like half a mile of jagged rocks before the sea went deep. It was too late to go back and we went on over shiny rock, with the dinghy going bump crash over the sharpest points. Everything was slippery and our fingers were numb with cold. When we got to what looked like a deep bit of water we all got in and the dinghy sat firmly on the bottom.

'We can't really afford to wait for the tide,' said Peter. So we all scrambled out and started again. This time the dinghy condescended to float in a wallowy way with little waves slopping over the stern. Peter and John tried to use the broken oar as two paddles, but we drifted steadily towards Kerrera. Then Michael said he would scull with the remaining oar. Dorothy and I had to hold him upright in the stern, one on each side – if the other two came further aft than the middle the sea came over the transom. Every now and then Michael would stagger and we would ship a little water.

After about half an hour the sky began to get a little lighter and we shook our dripping hair out of our eyes and looked at the time. 1700. Dorothy said, 'Could you put us down on the nearest bit of shore to Oban you can get, even if it's somebody's back garden?' John said, 'We're not putting you down anywhere until you've been back to our ship and had a drink to warm you up.'

Just as we bumped against the side of their ship the rain stopped and the sun came out. We went below to Peter's cabin and had tumblers of neat whisky. Then they rowed us ashore. The tide had gone down and we had to climb the side of a stone wall to reach the road. We then set out for Oban, steaming slightly in the sun and leaving wet footprints in the road, both talking very fast and not listening to each other. I watched Dorothy go swaying down the Pier to the Signal Station with a rolling gait, singing in snatches.

When I got back to Quarters I found that both my knees were right out of my only pair of silk stockings, and when I got undressed I was able to wring quite a lot of water out of my vest onto the floor of the cabin. My skirt and jacket took three weeks to dry over the stove at the Signal Station.

Joan said, 'Where on earth have you been?'

I said, 'Drinking whisky on a ship, with three officers.'

'Funny joke,' she said.

After so traumatic an afternoon of shared experiences, Peter Michael and John had arranged a date with us in town the next evening. But alas, the next morning early their ship sailed, and we never saw them again.

Nothing matched the enchantment of the first afternoon we walked to Gallanach, but from the practical point of view it was obviously a happy hunting ground for Getting on a Boat, so we set off the same way again a few weeks later. If nothing happened by the time we got to the ferry point we would go over to Kerrera on the ferry and get some eggs at the farm. The ferry was a small lopsided dinghy rowed by an ancient mariner who lived in a cottage on the beach the other side. When you turned the white board round to show its black side he came over and collected you if he happened to be looking. On Kerrera there was nothing, not even a path, just a large bare rocky island with the odd croft.

In the interval since our last expedition the rules and penalties from the First Lieutenant against Wrens setting foot on any kind of boat, or sailors allowing a Wren on any boat, had become even more dire, threatening Court Martial, instant dismissal from the Service with ignominy, and deportation to forced labour camp, for anyone who transgressed.

When we got as far as the ferry, Dorothy and I could see a large oiler anchored in Kerrera Sound. Alongside her was moored our old friend the patrol boat *Southern Star*, to whose signalman Alec we now flashed loving messages dozens of times a day and night. He must have been bored enough to be on the bridge watching the coast road through his telescope, because before you could say 'cutlass' all the crew were up on deck screaming, whistling, yelling, jumping up and down, and generally behaving in the way customary to males on a boat at the sight of a female. You would think they had been confined to a desert island for a year, instead of having steamed ten minutes out of Oban.

In a minute, a little dinghy with a Lieutenant rowing had pulled away from the side and was heading towards us, and quite soon we were sitting on a bunk in the Captain's cabin chatting and smoking. Dorothy did begin to say weakly, 'We're not supposed ...' and the Captain interrupted, 'no, neither are we, isn't it interesting?'

After a bit he said, 'Well, we've finished refuelling now, would you like a lift back to town?' So we sailed back to Oban pier on the bridge. Dorothy called up her Signal Station requesting a berth.

It was a highly successful beginning to the afternoon, though all too short. Thinking a little *bonne bouche* would round it off, we went straight on to North Pier, where the RAF Air Sea Rescue launches tied up their pinnaces. Quite soon we were whizzing out to an ASR launch, with an RAF Sergeant. He had come in from their base at Tiree. He was carrying an electric fire, which he was in the middle of mending. The previous night, he said, he had come into Oban and tried it out in a friend's room in the Great Western Hotel, where the RAF were billeted, and fused all the lights there. So he thought there might be something wrong with the wiring.

We were astonished to find how big the launch was. Apparently a crew of fifteen could live comfortably on it. Having seen over every inch, made tea in the galley, and inspected the engine room, we were forced to admit that, for non-Navy, it wasn't bad.

Right in front of the Signal Station at Ganavan, about a quarter of a mile off shore and half that distance long, was Maiden Island. It was a whale-shaped hump, low and green, a bit higher one end than the other. You could see why it was called Maiden Island – it was inviolable. Nobody had ever been on it because there was no way of getting there. All the ships going in and out of harbour went behind it, which meant that it was more often cursed than praised, as their signals disappeared for a bit until they came out the other side. We watched the gulls nesting there through the telescope, and sighed over our forlorn state, as inviolate in the Signal Station as was Maiden Island in the sea.

One afternoon the oncoming watch said, 'There must be a US Navy ship in the anchorage – there are some Yanks in town.' Joan and I scurried back to Quarters, changed our bellbottoms and seamen's jerseys for skirts and clean white shirts and, with Marian, who was also off watch, strolled with assumed nonchalance down the front. At North Pier was an impeccable, gleaming launch flying the Stars and Stripes. There was a crew of four US sailors on board, waiting to take their officers back from a conference in the Base.

'Hi girls,' they said, 'like a trip?'

We said, 'But what about your officers?'

'Aw hell,' one of them said, 'the Cap won't mind. Where would you like to go?'

There was only one answer. 'Maiden Island!' we said in unison.

The launch shot out of harbour and zoomed across Oban Bay. One of the Yanks had his arm around Joan and was saying, 'Gee babe, you're awful swell, we bin at sea four months, sure is good to see you.'

We zigzagged past Dunollie light and bumped on the rocks of Maiden Island. The three of us jumped ashore and scrambled on to the short turf. As we climbed ahead up to the highest point, 'Gee!' said the Yanks in voices of awe, 'black panties! They got black panties on!'

Up on the top rock we were waving like mad to the Signal Station. Soon the telescope shot out of the window and we could sense an apoplectic eye at the other end and imagine an incensed voice saying, 'They're on Maiden Island! With the Yanks!'

We jumped, with difficulty and another display of black panties, back into the launch, and they brought it round in a crisp curve towards the harbour. Joan's Yank was the fastest worker, but was having difficulties – he obviously wasn't used to dealing with a tiepin and tie, or a collar stud, and it slowed him up. 'Aw nerts,' he said as he pricked his finger on her tiepin.

As we approached North Pier, suddenly our hearts gave a hideous lurch. On the jetty stood eight of the US top brass, double omelettes of scrambled egg festooning their caps, gold braid up to the elbows, medals clanking across their chests. They were looking at their watches.

There was no time to jump overboard and swim ashore. Visions of the First Lieutenant shot though our heads. As the launch drew up alongside the jetty one of our sailors gave a cheery wave and shouted, 'Hi Cap! Get anything to eat?'

The grandest and most glamorous figure beamed back and said in a Gary Cooper drawl, 'Hi Hank! No hurry on our account.'

As we scrambled out of the launch he gave a glance at us, blinked, and then deliberately looked the other way. The other seven officers did the same, in a deadpan manner. They stepped down into the launch as though we had not existed, and we scurried up the jetty, praying that nobody was looking out of the window of the Base. We got away with it again. Though I was punished for quite meaningless crimes in Oban, I was never punished for the most heinous of all – Getting on a Boat.

5

Watchkeepers

'You lucky, lucky, girls,' said Dave sardonically, to the three of us who weren't on duty or in bed after night watch. 'Seven of you, for a three watch system. You've got a gash hand. God knows what you'll get up to with all that spare time.'

We were watchkeepers. There were no more weekdays and weekends for us until the end of the war. A three watch system worked like this:–

Day 1	0800-1300	1800-2300
Day 2	1300-1800	2300-0800
Day 3	Off	

There always had to be two of us on watch. In theory, with seven, we should have been able to switch around to relieve the monotony of doing night watch every third night for ever. But in practice we never even had a complement of six, because there was always more than one on leave, in Sick Bay, on loan to the Pier Signal Station, getting married, at Defaulters' Parade, on an exchange, or on an official trip somewhere. An odd number was better than an even, because it meant that we were not on watch with the same person *ad infinitum*, thus saving us from boredom, murder, and ultimate madness. For months at a time there were only five of us. There was never a time when we weren't doubling up watches because of some emergency or other. There was no let-up – no weekends off, and from Oban there was nowhere you could get to. In 1944 we didn't get any leave at all for six months, and then only a week. We could never go out for a day unless we went straight from night watch.

To Base we were apparently inexplicable. We got asinine messages saying, 'Only two of the watchkeepers have been at Squad Drill the last six weeks, will you ensure that all eight attend next week'. The polite answer was, two are always on the way on watch, two on the way back, and two asleep after night watch, and the other two if they weren't mythical would be doing all the other incidental chores so you are lucky to see any ever – we suggest you hold Squad Drill in the Signal Station. In effect, we tended to ignore all such messages in the hope that they would get lost in the welter of Admiralty documents silting up in the Station Hotel. Sometimes they did, but sometimes there was a boiling-up eventually.

One peculiar effect of the system was that we never got a proper cooked meal at the time it was served, which was 1300. On Day 1 we got back to Quarters at 1330, in time for the left-overs. On Day 2 we had to start for Ganavan at 1230, so we got a snack preview of the lunch at 1200. On Day 3 we were asleep or at least in bed, depending on how noisy it was, and we were forbidden to take food up to the cabin. They gave us sandwiches to take on night watch – sardine or spam – and some milk for tea.

Supper in Quarters was at 1730. It was a snack, very often cheese dreams. We got something dished up at 1700 on Day 1, mainly bread and marge, something left over at 1830 on Day 2, and on Day 3 we could get up at teatime and actually sit down to a meal with the rest of the Wrennery.

To the Quarters Petty Officer we were a nightmare, and to the cooks and orderlies a perpetual irritation. It wasn't their fault – we were all victims of a rigid system. Mealtimes in the Mess couldn't bend for watchkeepers, and watches couldn't be changed. The system was designed for the majority who worked daytime hours in office jobs, and was immutable. It was astonishing that we didn't get scurvy. Yet the problem of feeding watchkeepers must have been with the Navy since Canute. I often wondered what happened in the men's messes. For us, on £1 a week with everything rationed, there was no way of supplementing our diet, no food you could buy except canteen buns. Yet it never occurred to us to query the system. We continued to eat sardine sandwiches every third night. After a few months I always had indigestion.

We grew used to being a nuisance, always the scapegoats, always in the wrong place at the wrong time in the wrong clothes – coming to Divisions in bellbottoms, wearing blue shirts instead of white (they had soft collars attached, no studs, and washed a nice French navy, so were much sought after), in bed for inspection, missing at Squad Drill, up to mischief with the sailors in the middle of a respectable working day, flashing our lamps about on the Sabbath, even getting on a boat. People who had never been watchkeepers couldn't understand that we didn't do it on purpose – using up all the bath water at 1000, hanging sodden oilskins over the banisters at midnight, forever changing watches for some emergency unseen and unknown in Quarters so that we couldn't be Duty Orderly.

It had been enchanting, walking up to Ganavan for our first duty through the autumn afternoon, and walking back to Quarters in the dusk at 1800. It wasn't quite such fun turning out again at 2230, when everyone else in the Wrennery was going cosily to bed, with all our paraphernalia, and slogging along the coast road in the pitch dark. When an RAF truck came by, all bright lights and cheery bonhomie, we had to hurl ourselves into the ditch – the Navy didn't provide us with torches and you couldn't buy them. Coming back off night watch the coast road began to seem over-familiar, after doing it four times in 24 hours. Down into town we plodded, our eyes gummy with fatigue, past Glen Campa, putting on a spurt to get to Raasay Lodge before the orderlies cleared away the last of the breakfast at 0830. We dumped our gear in the hall and sat down dirty as we were, stuffing bread and bread and more bread after the night's bread, washing it down with strong tepid tea, with the orderlies clearing the tables round us and laying them up for lunch. We weren't hungry but we had to fill ourselves with all the available food to last us until the evening.

Once fed, we collapsed in a stupor of exhaustion in front of the newly-lit fire in the Common Room. Our feet, stuck into the grate in communal wellingtons, smelt horrible. The orderlies came and clucked round us with brooms and dusters and we sighed and gathered up our gear and staggered back up the road to Glen Campa. Here we climbed the stairs to our freezing cold damp cabin, dumped the gear, and collected towels and sponge bags. Then back to Raasay Lodge, up three floors to where there was a single bathroom, stripped off our smelly clothes and lowered ourselves in turn into water as tepid as the tea and about the same colour by the time we had both been in. We tried to drown the fleas as they swam off us, but fleas are a hardy race and only drown in very hot water. We then dressed again in our dirty clothes and tottered back up the road to Glen Campa, where we hung our sodden towels over the banister and crept into our icy beds.

By this time it was about 1000, and we dozed fitfully until about 1500 and then went down the town, shivery and empty and rather sick, to the YMCA, where we sat with buns and coffee until we started to thaw. After that there was nothing to do except go back to Quarters and eat cheese dreams for supper and go to bed again, but we could never sleep much after sleeping most of the day, and found ourselves waiting for the alarm to go at 0645 to start us on our 0800-1300 and 1800-2300 day.

Getting to Ganavan at 0800, we could never understand why the night watch couldn't be ready, and why with all night to play with they hadn't washed up and cleared the ashes and shaken the blankets. When it was our turn to be relieved at 0800, we could never understand why the day watch were so early and so bloody bright-eyed and bushy-tailed and censorious.

1800 to 2300 became the worst watch of all – the end of a very long day, and, with the weather deteriorating rapidly from autumn to winter, an increasingly unpleasant, not to say alarming, walk back at 2330, with the ghosts of early MacDougalls peering down from the ruins of Dunollie. We didn't seem to worry about flesh and blood lurkers in the undergrowth, and there never were any – it was too cold.

However, it began to be very wet, and the Lords of the Admiralty, in their charity, issued us with oilskins. We came back to Quarters one afternoon to find Marian and Joan stomping around the cabin stiff-legged in shiny black trousers. 'I can't bend my *knees!*' shrieked Marian. 'I can't sit!' 'You don't want to, you clot – you just want to walk to Ganavan.'

'I can't *walk* either – it's like being on stilts.'

The trousers were like a child's cardboard cutout, two dimensional, with no allowance for even a male bottom let alone a female.

'And the jacket – look – I can't bend my arms at all –.'

The jacket was similar in design, as stiff as sheet metal, with buttons which wouldn't go through the buttonholes. We had four pairs of trousers and four jackets between us – when we put them in the cupboard they stood up all on their own. We couldn't really wear them, they slowed us up so.

The next milestone in our progress was bicycles. As the weeks

67

went by we realised that we were not the only watchkeepers on the Ganavan road. Little Ganavan too worked a three watch system. Bert and Sid and Ern and Co. sheepishly overtook us on shiny RN bicycles, official numbers painted on the crossbars, their regulation blacked-out lamps shedding a welcome pencil of light on the inky road as they wobbled along.

'Dave,' said Carol, 'couldn't we have bicycles too? It isn't awfully nice, walking back so late.'

'Bicycles?' said Dave, 'My God girl, you'll be wanting Rolls Royces with chauffeurs next.'

However, the idea must have got round, because the next week Dave said laconically, 'You'd better collect your four bicycles this afternoon before I give them to somebody deserving. And don't let Jimmy the One know you've got them – he thinks Wrens' legs are made for walking, among other things.'

They're *men's* bicycles', said Marian when she saw them. 'And they're all rusty.'

'They're rather old,' I said dubiously, blowing the dust off one. They hadn't any of the shiny paint on, or any RN numbers.

'This one's got a puncture,' said Carol.

'They haven't got any lamps.'

'Mine hasn't got any brakes.'

'Dave …' we said.

'Now look here you lot, you ask for bicycles, and out of the kindness of my heart I get you bicycles. One more word and I'll take them away. And what is more, I'll tell you the story about the man who gave the girl a lift on his bicycle.'

'Tell us, tell us, Dave', we clamoured. We always felt that if we went on hearing the dirty stories the sailors told we'd begin to see the jokes eventually.

'When she got off, she realised it was a lady's bicycle,' said Dave.

Some of us saw the joke.

We pushed the bicycles up Oban front. A party of sailors fell about laughing when they saw us.

'Where's your maintenance rating?' they said.

'What do you mean?' we said.

'We have a rating on full-time maintenance work on *our* bicycles.'

'You mean – punctures and lamp batteries and brakes and all that?'

'All we have to do is ride 'em,' they said.

Back on the Ganavan road we now had to drag our bicycles with us down the ditch at night when the RAF transports passed. And on the downhill bit we had to dismount if the brakes didn't work. We rode them bumpily on the punctured tyres.

We did try to ride men's bicycles without brakes or lights, in oilskins which did not allow the knees or elbows to bend, but lacking the skills of circus performers we had to give up in the end and just resign ourselves to getting wet. I don't believe even a contortionist could get on and off a bicycle with a crossbar in oilskin trousers.

The end of the midnight rides came one evening when Marian staggered back to Raasay Lodge at 2100 clutching her cheek, with a sudden onset of raging toothache, leaving Pauline on watch alone for the last two hours. Carol and Rosemary relieved Pauline at 2300. At 2345, Pauline arrived back at Raasay Lodge screaming hysterically about a headless man in a kilt chasing her with a claymore all round the keep of Dunollie. She wouldn't stop screaming and they had to get the nurse from Sick Bay to give her an aspirin.

Dave got a rocket via the Wren Officers, who had been woken from their pristine slumbers. The powers that be decreed that our three watch system should now run:–

Day 1	0800-1300	1800-0800
Day 2	Off	
Day 3	1300-1800	

A fourteen hour night watch was far from ideal, and we still never got a proper lunch, but anything was better than the coast road at midnight in winter. We had all got the jitters by then.

69

6

Night Watch

Every third night was years and years long. One third night at 1800 Carol and Rosemary went off down the hill, and I was alone with Marian for fourteen hours. Unless anything momentous happened it would be a long and desperate battle to stay awake. We took down the Ensign and switched on Dunollie light. We logged the fishing boats out. We got the coal in. We made up the stove and made tea. We watched the sun sink over Mull in glorious Technicolor. We switched on the dark-shaded bulb over the log book, which was our only light. We ate some dank, cardboardy spam sandwiches. It was 1900.

We decided to split the night and try to get four hours' sleep each, Marian 2300-0300 and I 0300-0700. If your oppo. was a great friend, or had been ditched by her boy friend and spent the last three nights sobbing, or had a tummy ache, you crept around while she slept, and even did an extra hour (in cases of extreme devotion a whole night) and took her a cup of strong tea and a fried sardine sandwich in bed when you woke her. If you didn't like her you crashed around hurling coal in the stove and filling kettles to keep yourself (and her) awake.

Marian sewed straps on her vest and mended her knicker elastic and I knitted and we yawned and talked about food, and men, and what we would do after the war, which kept us awake until 2300. Then she went down the ladder and rolled into the smelly blankets on the bunk and I had four hours to get through.

It was as dark outside as the inside of a Highland Cattle. I propped the big telescope out of the fanlight and swung it very slowly round the whole expanse of sea from Dunollie to the seaplane base. There was not a glimmer of light. I might have been anywhere from the Arctic Circle to the Amazon jungle as far as my eyes were concerned. After a bit I began to feel as if I was blind-folded.

I pushed a writing pad under the small circle of dim light thrown on the counter from the black-encircled bulb and started a letter. Dear Mum – as millions of young people were writing just then all over the British Isles and Germany and Russia and China and Japan and America and Italy and indeed most of the globe – never guessing that she would keep all my letters and I would re-read them thirty-five years later. After every few minutes' writing I would go back to the telescope and swing it across the sea again. If I stopped writing to think, my eyelids would droop and my head would nod down onto the counter. It was so quiet. So quiet. It was midnight.

Not so quiet. There was the crack of a twig, soft footsteps on the steps outside. The handle of the door was tried. My heart thudded. A lighter shadow came round the open window by the telescope. A wheedling voice said, 'You all alone honey?'

I said, my voice coming out rather squeaky, 'No, of course not my chum's here, and – and – we're expecting an officer to arrive at any minute.'

That didn't cut much ice.

'Then how's about letting me come in just for a minute? I've kinda lost my way.'

'No, no,' I heard myself say, knowing that neither the lock on the signal room door nor the bolt on the back door downstairs would withstand determined pressure. 'You can't come in,' my voice was getting higher, 'it's all secret equipment here.'

'I sure am interested in anyone's secret equipment, honey,' drawled the voice. 'Here – Lucky Strikes.' A packet flopped on the counter.

'Yes, that's what I'm afraid of,' I said snappily. I could now distinguish the beautiful smooth pale beige cloth of the uniform, the US shoulder flash, the rather doughy clean-shaven jaw.

'Aw, c'mon honey, just for a minute, just to warm up,' he said, and turned his head sideways and pushed it through the fanlight. I suddenly swivelled the telescope inboard and the window fell smartly on the back of his crewcut neck. I thought he didn't look so nice with his head kind of squashed up sideways.

'I guess I'm sorta stuck, honey,' he said, baffled. I said coldly, 'Push the window up and you can get your head out.' He did and the window fell shut with a slam. I wedged it.

I could hear him muttering in a puzzled way as his feet retreated down the steps.

I took the binoculars and scanned the blackness outside

71

through the shut window. My teeth were chattering. I made some tea and was just about to bite into another sawdust sandwich when there was suddenly a scuffling sound and a curious muffled thud on the door downstairs. I opened my mouth to scream when the sound turned into a miniature galloping noise and a sheep shot luminously past below me and down the hill.

It was 0130. I finished my letter home. I decided to write a poem about the sunset, which had moved me to eloquence. Writing poetry kept me awake better than anything else. I wrote:

> The gulls in scattered fragments fly
> Haphazard in the evening sky,
> And drift like ashes floating by
> Upon the sea at Ganavan.
> No tender curve of breast or brow
> Can charm my dazzled senses, now
> My eyes have seen with rapture how
> The sun goes down at Ganavan.
> And as the purple shadows grow,
> The moonlight seems to spread and glow
> As if diffused from far below
> Upon the sea at Ganavan.

The sea was so dark outside I wondered if it was still there. The 'phone rang. 'This is the Duty Officer.' Sounding rather cautious. 'Are you on watch all night?'

'Yes, ma'am.'

'Are there two of you there?'

'Yes, ma'am.'

'Have you got the doors locked?'

'Yes, ma'am.' Long pause.

'Well, we don't want you to worry or anything but it's been reported that a German prisoner of war has escaped from a camp not far off. They think he's stolen a gun, and he's making for the coast. Last time he got out he killed a marine.'

'Yes, ma'am.'

'I just thought I'd mention it,' her well-bred voice tailed off apologetically, 'in case anyone does knock on the door – or anything.'

'Yes, ma'am,' I said. 'Thank you.'

'Be sure to let me know,' she said.

'Yes, ma'am,' I said.

I put the 'phone down. The Little Ganavan 'phone gave its husky ring. 'This is Bert. Have you just had a call from Base?'

'Yes,' I quavered.

'Well listen, loov, don't you fret, if you want anything joost ring us and we'll coom oop and settle the booger with our battleaxes. If you're scared we'll come now.'

'Oh thank you Bert,' I said, feeling quite feminine and protected for once. 'I'm fine, not a bit worried, but it's a marvellous offer.' I went down the ladder and wedged a chair under the outside door handle.

I went back to the telescope and the sea, turning my back firmly on the bleak hillside behind, bristling with little crouching bushes. There was nothing on the sea, not a flicker. I sat under the light bulb again and tried to learn a sonnet. I thought if I could learn one of Shakespeare's sonnets every night watch I might know them all by the end of the war. The war finished before I learnt them all, but it was an exercise I never regretted.

Like as the waves make towards the pebbled shore,
So do our minutes hasten to their end;

I closed the book of sonnets. It was 0215. Three quarters of an hour to go. My eyes started to close. My head drooped.

I jerked up. There was an extraordinary whining and groaning and scratching noise at the downstairs door, like hungry wolves. It didn't really sound like a German POW, unless he was a vampire, so emboldened by the proffered support of Little Ganavan I went out on the balcony with the Aldis and shone it down. Outside the door was a small bedraggled Scottish terrier. I went down and moved the chair and let it in, and carried it up the ladder under one arm. It wagged its tail frantically and started yapping. I put down a saucer of water and a sardine sandwich. It lapped up the water noisily, refused the sandwich with an injured air, wiped its beard all over the rolled up Ensign, growling, and settled down by the fire apparently for the night. It was wearing a smart tartan collar with no name.

I sat and thought in a bemused way. Then I 'phoned the Police Station.

73

'*Not* a Scottie with a tartan collar and no name? Very domesti-
cated?' said a weary voice. 'If so, it is always latching on to somebody new. We don't know who it belongs to.'

'What shall I do with it?' I said.

'My advice is, chuck it out again,' he said.

So I took it down the ladder and locked it out. It seemed to
bear no ill will, and scampered off.

It was 0230.

Half an hour to go, and the most terrifying ordeal of the night
approaching. I should have to go outside to the lav before I went
to bed. However petrified with fear we were, we never gave in and
used a bucket. The night the cat left a phosphorescent fish outside
the back door, Joan's screams could have been heard in Berlin.

I got coal up, made up the stove, raked out the ash, took the
kettle down to the galley and lurched up again with it full, to take
my mind off the urgent demands of my bladder. I had a last look
at the silent sea. Then it was time to wake Marian.

I shook the blankets and a tousled head emerged. She had taken
off her shirt, and as she turned over both shoulder straps exploded
apart against the strain of her bosom. She beamed owlishly at me.
'Wassermatter?' she said.

'Wakey, wakey,' I said. 'Had a good kip?'

'Heavenly,' she said. 'Dreamt I was in a gondola with a Polish
officer.'

'Did you hear anything?'

'No – why, did anything happen?'

'No, nothing happened,' I said.

'Good. Then can I mend my shoulder straps.'

'Will you hold the torch for me first?'

She stumbled to the door in her vest and blackouts and socks,
clutching the torch. I took a deep breath, shut my eyes, and
unlocked the door. As it swung open, all the demons of the night
skittered for cover. I ran the few yards into the blackened doorway
of the lav. There was no light in there and it smelt horrible. We
never cleaned it – we forgot in the day and were too terrified after
dark. In fifteen seconds I was back, and Marian made a dash, her
legs goose-pimpled with cold, while I held the torch from the
doorway in trembling hands. Then she pulled her bellbottoms
and jersey on and went up the ladder, and I went over to the bunk

and started to get into it. As soon as my head touched the pillow, I knew I should drop into a deep pit of sleep.

In the split second before my eyes shut, I heard the 'phone ring. Subconsciously I heard Marian's voice say, 'Yes ma'am – yes the signaller is in her bunk ma'am – yes I'll tell her ma'am.'

'I'm awfully sorry,' said Marian, coming down the ladder with one arm in her jersey and the other holding her shoulder strap up.

'Okay,' I said, sliding out of the clinging folds of my cover. 'I'll come – what is it?'

'It's Ops,' said Marian. 'They've just had a call from the RAF. There's a plane that's lost its way. They think it's somewhere over here. Could you go outside and point the Aldis at the sky and flash OBAN.'

'How long for?'

'She suggested until it gets light.'

'I wonder if I could tip the ten-inch up and signal on that?' I said, 'to save time.'

'If you do you'll have the whole Luftwaffe over, I should think,' said Marian.

'Should I go on the roof? Could he see better from there?'

'The officer said, could you get as near the sea as you could – then the pilot could identify the coastline. I don't think,' said Marian, 'she'd ever been up here.'

'Flaming hell,' I said, struggling into the communal duffel coat, 'I'm not going out on the cliff. After all, it's only *a plane*. It's not as if it was a ship.'

At 0500 a yellow eyelid showed in the sky over Ben Cruachan and the sun started to come up. We never heard any more about the plane. I went to bed.

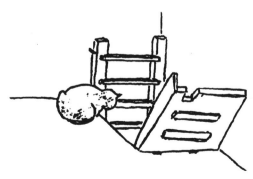

7

Blondie

Dave's sardonic voice came over the line at Ganavan one afternoon. 'Seeing as how I'm overflowing with the milk of human kindness, I thought I'd just mention that the Signal Officer WRNS is at this moment on her bicycle on the way out to inspect you.'

'Oh *thank* you Dave,' said Joan, who had answered the 'phone, knowing that, far more for his own sake than ours, the SO had better get a good impression or else. It was uphill all the way to Ganavan from the Station Hotel and we didn't know how athletic she was, but at the most we had about twenty minutes. There was a lot to do. Hide the dirty mugs and plates under the sink, remove Marian's bra, vest and pants from the clothes line over the stove, pull a blanket over the ever-unmade bunk, get coal in, make up the stove and throw the ashes over the cliff, put the kettle on, lock the CB's, which were propping up the chair leg, in the safe, enter something in the Log, plug the Aldis into a new battery, put our knitting and playing cards under the rug in the living room, 'phone Little Ganavan, odd members of whose establishment were now in the way of popping up for a cuppa char, and 'phone the men on Lismore and warn them to answer pronto if we signalled them.

We then did what we could with our appearance. We realised we had already drifted some way from the beautiful ideal of the honour of wearing Naval uniform, and were now dressed more for warmth and comfort than to conform with regulations. I had on a pre-war school sweater with frayed cuffs which had unsuccessfully been dyed navy from yellow, over a shrunk white pullover in which my father had once gone on a boat in 1912. My bellbottoms were shapeless and stained with coffee, and my toes were sticking through a pair of ancient plimsolls. Joan was wearing bellbottoms and a fluffy pink angora jumper and very old silver sandals. We had to settle for freezing, and strip off to the rolled-up shirt sleeves – we were not allowed to roll down our shirt sleeves unless we were wearing jackets. We hoped the bellbottoms would cover our feet if we stood with bent knees.

Ganavan, being so primitive that it was near to self-sufficiency, brought out the worst of our instincts for survival at an age when they are frighteningly strong anyway. Every lump of coal we carried warmed us and boiled our kettle. We became ever more selfish, anarchic, ruthless and intolerant. We had abrogated responsibility for civilisation and handed it over to the Navy – we just had to look after ourselves if we wanted to survive. Quarters was where we lived officially, but Ganavan had become home – our castle. We were not detached from the war, and we were passionately patriotic, but this was our own part of the struggle and from Ganavan we ran it.

When we paused to look through binoculars at the coast road, we were only just in time. A large blonde woman could be seen sitting upright and dignified on a bicycle with a basket on the handlebars. She pedalled floatily along, overflowing a little like a feather mattress, then went out of sight behind the cliff.

We were always at an advantage in welcoming visitors, as they were so out of breath from the climb. As she came panting up the outside ladder we sprang prettily to our feet in confusion at being interrupted in filing signals, and said, 'Good afternoon ma'am,' thinking that a salute would introduce an unnecessarily formal note.

'I'm Second Officer Baines,' she gasped, when she got her breath back. She looked round with an acute eye. 'It's very tidy – did anyone tell you I was coming?'

'Oh no, ma'am,' we said, shocked.

At that point a diversion occurred when the patrol boat called us up. I seized the lamp and answered. The signalman said, 'Is Carol on watch?'

'What is it saying?' 2/O Baines said to Joan.

Light dawned on me and I realised that the Officer didn't know morse. I sent back 'No, go to hell,' to the patrol boat, and said to the Officer, 'Am returning to harbour at 1800 hours'.

Then, as now, a Signal Officer who couldn't read morse signals appeared to me an anachronism of the first water, like a pilot who couldn't fly. We bent our merciless intolerance on all such.

We showed her over the Signal Station. We even showed her the filthy blankets in the cabin, which had been slept in by generations of sailors, and the grey greasy pillows, and suggested that it would be nice if they were cleaned or if new ones were issued. 'You'd better ask your Quarters PO,' she said. 'We have,' we said, 'and she says the issue of supplies to Ganavan is nothing to do with Quarters.' 'Oh dear,' she said, 'well, I'll have to see what I can do in Base.'

That was the last we heard of it. The Navy never solved the problem of who was responsible for our supplies. I eventually stole a calico mattress cover which I jealously guarded and used as a sleeping bag until the end of the war. It was never washed, but at least it only smelled of me.

We mentioned that carrying buckets of coal and batteries up the cliff was not very good for our insides. She said, 'I must speak to Jimmy the One about that.' We knew what good that would do.

Feeling a sense of anti-climax, we gave her a cup of tea.

'And do you signal to Lismore?' she said.

I took the Aldis over to the side window facing the island and, praying that Fred hadn't gone back to sleep, flashed him up. He answered before I had finished the call sign.

She was beside me, jumping up and down like a little girl in a way that didn't really become someone with a bosom, and saying, 'I saw it! I saw it! What is it saying?'

Fred was saying, 'Has the old trout come yet?'

'*Southern Wave* leaving for Dunstaffnage,' I tactfully invented.

'It's on the cards,' she said, 'you'll go there one day.'

'To *Lismore*? said Joan.

'Yes – eventually the signalmen there will probably go to sea, and you'll take over.'

'What, and *live* there?'

'Oh yes – you'd probably have a cook.'

We were stunned into silence. We wouldn't even have to live on boiled seaweed or whatever Carol and Rosemary were experimenting with in the food line at the time.

'As a matter of fact,' she said, '2/O Patterson had arranged a boat for you to go out there for a day, last week, but the First Lieutenant vetoed it.'

We digested this.

'Would you *want* to go?' she said. 'Life would be hard there, and boring.'

'Oh ma'am,' we breathed, forgetting all our loyalty to Ganavan, 'more than anything else in the world.'

'Well, I'll tell 2/O Patterson,' she said.

When she had gone, I trained the big telescope on Lismore and drew it slowly along the low green length of the island. When the convoys came in, you couldn't see the shore for liberty ships, their forests of rigging blotting out the sky. But today the anchorage was empty, and it was a desert island.

'Imagine,' said Joan, 'living on a real island.'

'No Jimmy the One,' I said.

'No Squad Drill; no Church Parade.'

'Real food.'

'No Signal Officer.'

'No Dave.'

From then on, we were lost in a dream of Lismore. It was four miles away, ten miles long, and a mile wide. It had a rough track from end to end, a church in the middle, a pier half way along one side and a quay half way along the other, a few crofts, and Lady Rock lighthouse at the south end. We hadn't the faintest idea what life there would be like, but we fell for the glamour, and with the egocentricity of youth we already felt it belonged to us. We never ceased to complain of the privations of Oban, and there was no doubt that life on Lismore would have involved us in even more excruciating discomfort and boredom, but we saw it in a golden haze. We couldn't wait for the men there to go to sea.

'They say its name means Little Garden,' said Joan.

'We've absolutely got to get there,' I said.

8

Lismore

Dorothy 'phoned from the Pier Signal Station. 'I've been talking to the skipper off one of the drifters. He's going up to Ballachulish on Tuesday morning, if the weather's fit, and coming back late afternoon. He could drop us off on Lismore. Can any of you get off watch for the day?'

Dorothy and Rosemary were off watch, and Joan and I managed to switch and get a free day. It was mid-November, and for once the fates smiled on us and there was a cold, brittle cleanness, with sparkling sea and golden hills. Even the pier looked less sleazy than usual, with the sun reflecting rainbow lights from the puddles of oil.

We had to climb over five drifters to get out to the *Margaret Jane*. We sailed at midday. The first thing the skipper said was, 'Ye'll want some food – go below, the lads are heating some soup. It'll be too cold for ye on deck.'

It was warm and cosy in the little cabin and the soup was delectable, but we didn't want to waste a moment of the majestic scenery unrolling overhead, and soon we were up on deck, hanging over the side, spellbound. The mountains which encircled Oban were covered in snow, and the sounds and lochs looked like pictures of Norway. The sea was deep green and glittering, the sky a light icy blue, the snow-covered mountains rising on every side, and the green hump of Lismore steadily getting nearer.

At 1300 the *Margaret Jane* bumped in beside the jetty and we swarmed up the ladder and waved goodbye to our skipper as the drifter steamed away again.

It was so quiet we found ourselves walking on tiptoe, and greener and less rocky than the other islands we had been on. On a flat stretch of grass by the landing stage were three nissen huts and a long low white cottage. There was no sign of life. On a little hill above was the signal station, with another nissen hut beside it. It was like going from Lilliput to Brobdignag, to see them so big after looking at them so small through a telescope from Ganavan. We followed a pebbly track which wound up the hill, and knocked on the green painted door of the signal station. Nobody answered so we went in.

A lean and lugubrious looking sailor was sitting on a stool by the window reading a very large book with very small print. Another sailor was sitting in the corner with his back turned. Neither looked up.

Dorothy cleared her throat and said, 'Hallo, we're from Ganavan.'

The studious sailor looked up very slowly. He put a finger in the pages of his book and took off his glasses. It seemed to take a long time for him to take it in that we were real.

I said chattily, 'We've come over for the day in the *Margaret Jane*. Did you ever work at Ganavan?'

After a long pause he said hesitatingly, 'Well, no, you see I'm not very strong and I could never have stood the toughness of the life there. That's why they sent me here.'

Joan said, 'Are you busy?'

He swung his head round and blinked at her. 'I don't know really. We just live here.'

Rosemary said, 'What's the food like?'

He said vaguely, 'We don't go down to the camp on the beach much. It's all right I think. More or less like my mum cooks. Lots of rice pudding.'

My mouth watered at the thought. I loved rice pudding – I could never get enough. It was the only thing that filled me up.

The signal station wasn't like ours. It was so clean for one thing, and better built, but the telescopes and lamps were not so good as ours.

I said, 'Do you often come to Oban?'

There was a long pause. Then he addressed the hunched back of the other sailor. 'When did I go to Oban, Alf?'

'What, Jim?' Alf turned half round. 'Must have been – yes – when I came back from leave you went in for an afternoon. That would have been beginning of August.'

'It rained,' said Jim. 'When I got there I waited on the pier till the boat went back.' There was a long pause. 'I don't like Oban,' he said. He was becoming quite loquacious with a bit of practice.

He jerked his head at Alf. '*He* has to go in every two-three months for his silks.'

We looked baffled.

Alf got up and pulled a newspaper parcel out of a locker and flung it down on the counter. He jerked his thumb towards it and went back to his corner.

When we gingerly unwrapped it, out fell a bundle of the most beautiful embroidered mats we had ever seen. They were worked in glowing colours and were like Chinese mats, with silky fringes and tassels and rosettes of flowers. As we exclaimed in delight, the back of Alf's neck went pale pink.

A silence fell and Dorothy caught my eye and said, 'I think we'd better go for our walk now.'

Jim said, 'When you come back, go to the cookhouse down by the beach and they'll give you tea.'

Before we were out of the door, he had opened his book again, and Alf was bent over his embroidery in the corner.

As we passed the nissen hut behind the signal station we could see a glowing stove and four spotless beds.

We set off along the track which ran like a spine up the island. It was bitterly cold, but in a dry brittle way that was exhilarating, and with the brisk exercise we glowed and felt like singing. The grey expanse of time in Oban seemed to roll off us. We were the only people in the world, frozen in eternal youth. There were little streams, thick with cresses, running through the grass. When we paused and listened the silence was complete.

We came to a little oblong building which we found was the church. 'Just think,' said Rosemary, 'we could come here on a Sunday.' We saw ourselves kneeling purely in the pews, the crofters touching their forelocks as we came out, leading the idyllic life. It was our promised land.

Dorothy had managed to get a film and took a photo of us. There the three of us are, sitting on a grassy bank beside a little waterfall, with our arms round each other's shoulders, wearing jumpers and skirts and naval money belts, looking at once vulnerable and egocentric, and full of dreams and nervous energy. How could we have believed for a minute that Lismore would satisfy our complicated desires? We were lucky to identify the unattainable with an actual place, for a little while.

When we came running back to the jetty, the sun was getting low and glittering in a steel path on the sea. The cook was looking out for us, and had a huge tea ready – freshly caught fish fried to a turn, newly baked bread, butter, raspberry jam, syrup, cheese and, did we want any more, there was plenty.

The rest of the sailors joined us, and then showed us round. We exclaimed at the luxury and cleanliness. The nissen huts were beautifully equipped, with polished floors, bright woolly rugs, pastel walls and chintzy curtains. There were easy chairs, wireless sets, comfortable beds, shelves, cupboards, and glistening white baths and basins. Everything was swept and polished meticulously. You couldn't believe it was in the same world as the Wren Quarters in Oban.

When the *Margaret Jane* chugged in at 1700 and we jumped on board and sailed away, our last glimpse of Lismore was of the sailors leaping about kicking a football on the tussocky grass by the shore. They were laughing a lot, looking so clean-limbed and light-hearted that they seemed a different race from the dim figures skulking the dark streets in Oban, with nothing to do but wolf-whistle.

The skipper said, 'Ye must come into the wheelhouse – it'll be company for me.' So we sat back on cushions while he leant carelessly on the wheel, smoking a pipe, and gazing out. The sun slowly set, and the calm cold sea was as smooth as silk, stretching away to where the mountains glimmered in the distance. It was silent except for the beat of the engine and the sea lapping against the side. We were lulled into a dream, and listened lazily to the skipper's voice, very deep and Scottish, telling us about his daughter who was a nurse and his three sons in the Navy.

As we went past the Signal Station, the skipper said, 'Why don't you call up your friends on watch?'

Dorothy picked up the lamp and flashed, 'Hallo – it's us coming back from Lismore.'

The morse which shot back had a slightly hysterical tone. 'Terrific flap on here all day – U-boat sighted – can you come straight out, fire's out, bring up some coal with you, ten-inch lamp burnt out.'

Joan and Rosemary jumped off the *Margaret Jane* and went up through the town at a gallop towards Ganavan. Dorothy went off to the Pier Signal Station, and I wended my way more slowly back to Quarters.

Florence, the Chief Officer's Steward, was sitting on the window seat in the Mess.

'Oh Florence,' I said, 'we went to Lismore and it was so *heavenly* there, we absolutely *must* work there.'

'You'd better forget it,' she said. 'They'll never let you go. And it wouldn't work – you're none of you ready for that sort of life. You are too conscious of time passing,' she said.

'I don't know what you mean,' I said.

They stalled, in Base, about sending us there. Then, after D-Day, the war was getting stale and I suppose it wasn't worth the trauma.

So I never went to Lismore again.

9

The Cabin

Late in the autumn, the Quarters Petty Officer said one day, 'We're going to move all seven of you into one cabin in Raasay Lodge.' The three of us who saw the prospect of stamping the ice of Glen Campa off our frozen feet for the last time were pleased. We should be able to have a bath and go to bed after night watch without getting undressed twice and risking pneumonia. And there was hot water in Raasay, and a fire in the Common Room. The four who had been in Raasay all along took our advent, and the prospect of sharing a cabin for eight, philosophically.

The euphemistically entitled cabin was a large oblong attic room on the second floor. We had to creep up the stairs past the first floor where the Joan Hunter Dunn officers slept in their large single rooms. Against the high pitch-pine staircase wall at the second bend hung a huge motheaten tiger skin, an animal presumably slain in the environs of Raasay Lodge with a hauberk. We used to twitch its ear as we went past, to make clouds of dust swirl round the stairs.

I misguidedly picked the bed by the window, thinking I would like to sit up in bed and see the sea. The window, which was under one of the gables, had a sash which rattled and did not fit properly. Once, I came in and found my bed covered in snow. (They said it didn't ever snow in Oban, but it did while I was there.)

There were six other beds – no double bunks, for which we were very grateful. Between every two beds was a chest of drawers with four drawers, and a wooden chair. There was a second window on the side wall, which, with the fireplace (blocked by a chest of drawers) and the door, ensured a good healthy through draught from all points of the compass. There was of course no heat. We stuck our pin-ups over our bedheads to indicate ownership, emptied our cases into two drawers each, and paused to consider The Cupboard.

The Cupboard was a massive fixture which took up all the wall opposite the window. Heaven knows what monstrous Scottish gear it had been designed to house, as surely only the under-skivvies could have been persuaded to occupy so bleak an attic. It was a gift to us. Into it and on top of it went everything, and as time went on it silted up so that the doors wouldn't shut properly.

Somehow the cabin never got cleaned. We missed out at rounds and inspections because there were always two watchkeepers asleep there, and the black cotton curtains drawn across, so most of the time we lived on tiptoe in a twilight murk. We didn't have to see sufficiently well to identify heavy clothing, as it was communal, like nuns' – we just pulled the nearest and least smelly wellingtons and the oilskins with the smallest rents out of the cupboard and thrust them back when we had finished with them.

In time we embarked on various unconsummated hobbies and pushed the bodged-up fruits to the back of the cupboard. It was too cold for perishables to smell as they decayed. Like us, they remained in a semi-refrigerated state.

Here, for eighteen months, we shared our joys and sorrows – opened a letter and burst into tears, snuffled with colds and tummy aches, talked in our sleep, sweated out fourteen days Confined to Barracks (the standard punishment), darned and mended and undid food parcels, set each other's hair, had crazes for doing slimming exercises, and dreamed about home, and leave, and men and what we would do when the war was over.

Occasionally the Quarters PO would say, 'Have you cleaned your cabin this week, girls?' and we would righteously reply, 'Of *course* Chiefie,' and just for the look of it take a broom up and sweep some of the fluff, from round the beds, under the chests of drawers, so that it didn't swirl round in swathes every time the door opened.

One morning Nemesis caught us. A new Duty Officer arrived, a keen type with a thin nose and eagle eye. Joan was dozing after night watch, and I was in bed leaning on one elbow trying to read a letter from my sister in the dim light from the shrouded window. 'Today there were some bombs near the school and they sent us home early,' she wrote. 'I am being taught to serve overarm.' Marian was sitting on her bed in the dark, sewing on a suspender, and Peggy was tinting her hair and singing tunelessly 'I'll be seeing you, In all the old familiar places, That this heart of mine embraces, All day through.' Her breath came out in a frozen cloud.

By then we had grown acclimatised to the penetrating cold, to our blue chapped hands and our socks stuck to our toes with broken chilblains.

We heard Chief's voice outside the door. 'You can't go in there, ma'am.'

'Why not?' said a carrying voice.

'It's the watchkeepers' cabin. They're asleep.'

'I can still inspect it, can't I? Stand back please.'

Firm steps clanked across the boards, the curtains were swung back, and we and the cabin were revealed in the brutal light of day. Suddenly we were conscious of what it must look like to an outsider. As the officer wrestled to raise the sash window (which had a broken cord and was stuffed up with letters round the edge) and a blast of icy air blew in, the fluff rose and swirled like a blizzard. There were sticky rings and dirty cups cluttering up the tops of the chests of drawers, which were thick with dust. Rather tatty pin-ups flapped on the walls. There were bits of a bicycle Carol had tried to mend all over the floor.

Joan and I sat up in bed gaping like baby sparrows. Peggy's hand was arrested with a hairpin raised defensively. Marian's needle was frozen through her suspender.

'And *what*,' said the officer, 'is in here?' With a dramatic gesture she hauled open the doors of The Cupboard. This sudden movement was too much for the top shelf, which was a bit rocky. There was a noise like the finale of the 'Hall of the Mountain Kings' and a cascade of Things hurtled out and crashed about her. All the oilskins and wellingtons, dozens of packets of ST's (we had a free issue of a packet a month and never used them all so they accumulated), half a very old pie in a piedish (Carol and Rosemary had gone to cookery classes for a bit at one stage), bundles of old copies of *Picture Post* and *Lilliput* and *Picturegoer*, lopsided pots (they had tried to learn pottery), bags of maggotty apples, a mouldy cake, three solid bottles of milk, several green pots of marmalade, and worst of all, six very dirty plates from the Mess with the coagulated remains of rice pudding, stew, baked beans, and kipper clinging to them. We were not allowed to remove any plates of food from the Mess.

Visible among the raincoats and greatcoats and tiddley jackets and old bellbottoms and seamen's jerseys and odd items of civilian

87

clothing which were rammed into the bottom half of The Cupboard were cocoa-stained cups and saucers, eggy knives and forks, dog bowls and cat bowls containing ancient remains of unidentifiable meat and fish (Carol and Rosemary had kept a cat in the Signal Station, and two dogs in succession – they had all given us fleas and eventually disappeared after bouts of spoiling and neglect, probably shot by a shepherd), tennis racquets, fishing nets, balls of wool and half-knitted jumpers, and bits of seaweed and moss and shells people had collected. We held our breath in case any of the mice scampered out, but they had obviously realised that discretion was the better part of valour.

It was awful, unforgivable, and we quaked, knowing there was only one punishment for such an offence.

'Fourteen days CB,' said the Officer crisply. 'And, Chief, this cabin is to be inspected by you personally every morning at 1000 until further notice.'

Considering the rocket Chiefie must have got, she behaved with great charity. More in sorrow than anger, 'Oh, girls, girls, I have *asked* you,' she came back and said, wringing her hands.

Fourteen days CB was a not unacceptable punishment in winter. There wasn't anywhere to go when we were off duty, and we got plenty of fresh air and exercise getting on duty and back.

Chiefie did inspect the cabin every day for three weeks. Then a measles epidemic gave her too much to think about. There was an effective grapevine, and any plan by the officer to inspect us again was conveyed to us in advance.

In six weeks we were well on the way to creating a comfortable slum again on the second floor. Carol had taken up and dropped basket weaving, and there were coils of cane left soaking in an old rusty leaking zinc bath in the middle of the floor.

10

The Others

The seven of us were not all V/S Wrens. There were never enough V/S Wrens to go round. Our training was comparatively long and intensive, but although we didn't know it our usefulness to the Navy was short lived, having a peak period before and immediately after D-Day. By the end of 1944 sailors were coming back to shore jobs again, and by early 1945 many of the war-time shore signal stations were closing down. We took over at Oban in October 1943, and the Signal Station closed in February 1945.

It was not worth training too many of us, so we were supplemented by other category Wrens, who had had shorter training or none at all. They took down the signals as we read them, and we taught them telephone and message procedure. We started at Ganavan with five signallers, and two SDO Wrens, who had had basic training in the Signal Distribution Office. The system worked fairly well. The signallers had to take responsibility, and could only sleep on night watch if the unqualified Wren was reliable enough to watch for ships entering and leaving harbour and wake her up to give the challenge.

On the fourteen-hour night watch, we usually each reckoned to get a few hours' sleep in the cabin below the signal room, but while the unqualified Wren enjoyed untroubled slumber, the V/S Wren was roused a number of times by a voice wailing down the hatch, 'There's a ship flashing – you'll have to come up!'

You taught them to send 'A S' in morse on the Aldis – the 'wait' signal – while you crawled out of the grey flea-ridden blankets and up the ladder, losing the fuggy heat it had taken you so long to generate. Unless it was below zero you had taken off your bellbottoms before getting into the bunk, and there was no time to struggle into them. You stood in the dark signal room on an Aldis box for height, with the fanlight propped open for the lamp and telescope and a howling gale whistling round your goose-pimpled thighs between your navy blue blackouts and your navy blue socks. 'R', your shivering fingers fumbled out on the Aldis

– 'receiving you'. It had better be important. Wavering and trembling as the boat rocked, the morse came back, 'Is Carol on watch?'

This happened so often it became a standard joke. 'Can't you stop them calling you up at night?' we said to Carol. What was it about her that made her the prime target for their nocturnal confidences? I was so furious one night when I had to get up three times to answer the same query from different ships that when I got back to Raasay Lodge in the morning I wouldn't speak to her at all.

Next night she was on watch. In the morning I was peacefully making up my sleep in the cabin when someone stormed in and pulled the bedclothes off me. 'Three times,' an apoplectic voice shouted. 'Three times last night! Is Stephanie on watch!' It was Carol.

Carol and Rosemary, who were both V/S, did everything together and were nearly always on watch together. Marian was not a signaller but she got to know so much about what we did that we almost thought of her as one. Joan was V/S, and usually on watch with Marian. Of the three of us who joined them from Glen Campa, Pauline and I were signallers and Peggy was SDO. But we were never a static community for long, we were like the ten little Indians.

Peggy went off for a weekend, to get married to her sailor sweetheart in Birmingham. We were slightly in awe of her when she returned. She was now in a different category of human being.

'Laugh,' she said, 'you'd have died! Every bit of glass blown out of the shop window downstairs the night before, and it had only been in a week!'

'Did you have a honeymoon?' I said, thinking about palm trees and balconies and satin dresses and violins.

''Course we did', she said. 'Mum and Dad moved out of their bed and slept on the settee. But we didn't get much sleep because of things in the bed.'

'Things in the bed?'

'Hairbrushes, boots, saucepans, our pyjamas sewn up, and all the kids on the landing outside looking through the keyhole and giggling. It was the funniest night I ever had! In the morning Joe had to get a train at eight back to Liverpool, so we didn't have time for breakfast.'

I looked at her wedding ring and thin single diamond engagement ring thoughtfully. A lot of different emotions struggled in me. Envy, and curiosity, and anger, and repugnance, and something else I couldn't quite define – a sort of glimmering of an idea that Peggy was set to be one of the winners in life, because she accepted things as they came and had no false expectations.

Later on Joe got posted to Rosyth and Peggy was drafted to married quarters there.

'What will you do after the war?' I asked her when I saw her off.

'Joe and I will go back and help Dad in the shoe shop, if it's still standing,' she said. 'We'll do up the attic room. If Joe comes through the war, of course.'

And if he doesn't, I thought, you'll go back there on your own, and being married will be like a dream that didn't happen, but you won't hold it against anyone, you'll just get on with life.

Pauline's bed was opposite mine, so I got the full benefit when she sat up in the middle of the night with her eyes tight shut pointing at me and wailing in a dramatic voice, 'A ship! I can see a ship!' She worried a lot – she was conscientious. She tried to Look on the Bright Side and Make the Best of Things. It was being conscientious that made her carry two Aldis batteries up the cliff to the Signal Station at a gallop in torrential rain. When she got into the signal room, she lay on the floor and started crying. 'It hurts, it hurts,' was all she would say.

We gathered round. Her sobs turned to screams.

'It's rheumatism,' said Rosemary.

'I think it's something broken in her inside,' said Marian.

'I expect,' said Joan detachedly, looking down at her, 'she'll never be able to have any children.' Our knowledge of gynaecology and obstetrics was minimal. We watched her as she writhed.

'She could get a draft South,' I said.

She did.

Marian, who was placid, went on knitting and darning and sewing on suspenders and writing down the signals as we read them to her. She was hopeless about time. Once when someone said, 'Aren't you *nearly* ready?' she replied with great dignity, 'I'm *always* nearly ready,' and that became her nickname.

Joan was a realist. Like me, she knew that basically life was awful and unredeemable and that the worst always happened and was worse than your direst imaginings; that every cloud had a darker lining and that if one door shut the next slammed in your face knocking your teeth in, and that the only answer to the person who adjures you to Look on the Bright Side is 'Why?'

She was accident-prone and had dramatic illnesses. She went on watch at 1300 with Marian in rude health. When Pauline and I arrived to relieve them at 1800 we found Joan covered from head to foot with huge red spots and with her face swollen like a football. She was dripping with sweat and obviously had a high temperature. When the spots had come out about tea-time, Marian had 'phoned Sick Bay and asked if she could bring Joan straight along there at 1800 when they came off watch. The MO said, 'Oh I can't wait to see anyone after 1730, I'm going out. You'll have to go back to Quarters for the night and report in the morning.'

Marian 'phoned Quarters to warn them, and the Petty Officer said, 'I'm not having her inside the door so you needn't try.'

Marian 'phoned the Nursing Sister in the Base and she said, 'If the MO can't see her nobody else can.'

We stood and looked at Joan, shivering and sweating and blotched with spots which were coming up in droves as we watched. Even in that parlous state, she still looked languishing and gracefully droopy, like Camille or La Belle au Bois Dormant.

'She can't stay here,' I said. 'And anyway look, there's a ship flashing.'

When I had dealt with the ship I found that Joan and Marian had staggered off down the hill and could be seen cycling very slowly along the coast road. Later Marian rang up.

'We went to Sick Bay,' she said, 'and said we were going to sit there until someone saw Joan. After two hours they got the MO back, from a party I think. He said she'd got acute ptomaine poisoning.'

'Well, thank goodness she'll get treatment,' I said. 'Will she be in long?'

'She's not in,' said Marian. 'The nurse gave her a bottle of calamine lotion and sent her back to Quarters. Chiefie was mad, but she couldn't do anything. And anyway, Joan is Duty Orderly tonight, until 2300.'

When Peggy went, we got June. June fell in the harbour one

night in December. She was a chubby, trusting girl, like a nice puppy, with a smile that curled the corners of her mouth right up. She was on loan to the Pier Signal Station, as Sue, who had been so thrown at the sight of Highland Cattle, had developed asthma and been drafted South.

June was doing the night watch, and about 2300 the Duty Officer at Base 'phoned and asked her to come over and collect a hand signal and deliver it to a ship moored alongside the pier. June was so short that her oilskin coat touched the ground all round, so that she looked like Mrs Noah. She beamed at the Officer as she collected the signal, her hat clamped to the back of her head over a mop of fair curly hair. Down to the pier she trotted, with her wellingtons going slip-slop through the puddles, and stepped in a pool of diesel and shot over the edge.

It was a long way down, but she was so surprised she didn't have time to scream. Afterwards she always swore she remembered going under three times, but we assured her she was so plump she must have just bounced, because she still had her hat on. A sailor on the nearest drifter fished her out with a boathook, and she was dumped on the pier, redolent of diesel and cod. The oilskins and wellingtons had fallen off.

Back she padded in her socks and duffel coat to Base, and knocked on the Officer's door. The Officer was on the 'phone and shouted 'Come in' without looking up. 'Please ma'am,' stuttered June through chattering teeth, 'I'm afraid I couldn't deliver the signal.' 'Whyever not?' said the Officer irritably, and then hearing a heavy dripping noise looked up and beheld June.

We were asleep in Quarters when there was a sudden commotion. We could hear June coming up the stairs, talking nineteen to the dozen at the top of her voice. She was half led and half carried in by the MO and the nurse, pushed into bed and held forcibly down.

'Quick!' shouted the nurse. 'Run a bath, as hot as you can! And one of you get dressed and go over to Sick Bay and ask for The Hot Water Bottle!' It was the first we knew that such a thing existed in the whole of Oban, except for the ones the officers had. We thought they had become extinct. 'And ask Chief to put some bricks in the oven!' she added.

June's voice was still going on, getting higher and higher,

until they rammed a thermometer in her mouth. 'Don't answer her,' hissed the nurse, 'severe shock – hypothermia – dangerous condition ...'

We didn't think there was much wrong with June. When the MO and the nurse had gone, having packed her round like something in a haybox and doped her with aspirin, we started asking her all about it.

'It's the wellies,' was all she would say in a drowsy voice, 'I borrowed them from Ted, they were much too big, and now they're in the drink and he'll be furious.'

'Wasn't it awfully *cold*?' said Joan.

'Oh Joan, said June reproachfully, looking at her with soulful eyes, 'think of the sailors – in the open boats.'

11

Raasay Lodge

Now that I slept and ate in Raasay Lodge, I began assessing it in more detail – discovering the sharp corners and jagged edges in the struggle for existence there, and padding myself out metaphorically to evade or endure, since it seemed I could not escape.

Opposite the cabin was a small bathroom containing a lavatory, a bath, and a basin, which was for the use of all the Wrens on that floor. Inadequate pieces of thin blackout curtain were looped with safety pins on strands of wire round these three essential objects, and within this space three or four of us at a time would jockey for position. The water was never hot. I became disenchanted with this bathroom after one of the Wrens who used it went into Sick Bay with scabies. Ever since then, when away from home, I have stepped straight from the bath into my slippers, having dried my feet on the edge of the bath first. Somehow I just cannot fancy other people's bath mats, however clean the people appear to be. I didn't like the blackout curtain either, wrapping itself around my dripping form as I dried myself in the bath.

Fortunately I discovered a bath block which had been built out at the back of Raasay Lodge into the vegetable garden. At the risk of seeing Auld Hamish's face peering through the window, one could get a hot bath there. I can't imagine where the hot water came from, unless it was a secret spring or piped from the South of England. The walls, ceiling and floor were bare concrete, dripping wet with condensation and covered in curious fungi, and there was a duckboard on the floor which I didn't tread on with bare feet. However, the water was hot enough to drown the fleas, and after night watch I used to run across the Common Room and up two flights of stairs and across the cabin into bed without all the warmth wearing off.

Also at the back was a vast laundry where we did our dhobi-ing. It was even safe to haul garments up to the ceiling – they didn't air, only got damper, but morale was comparatively high in Raasay Lodge and ironed clothes didn't get stolen as they did in larger Bases.

In the laundry there were enormous rusty mangles propped up in corners, and dusty trestle tables, and what looked like siege engines from Flodden Field. Chiefie had never been able to make much progress in tidying up the laundry, which was just as well as it came in handy for the odd disorganised job like plucking and trussing a chicken. I had never done that before, but a man in a farm cottage offered me one still warm when I was going on leave, and the invaluable Florence showed me how to deal with it. It looked much smaller when she had finished, rather stringy in fact, and it went nicely into my respirator case for the journey home. I don't know who cleared up the feathers in the laundry.

Next to the Common Room was the Mess. It was an oblong room with a bay window and a window seat looking out into the windswept, rainlashed bay with seaplanes bobbing up and down opposite. One long table ran down the length of the room.

On the short wall opposite the window was a large sideboard. As we entered, our eyes automatically went first to the sideboard, where the letters were laid out. Letters from Mums and Dads and sisters and brothers, fiancés and husbands, Air Mail from boy friends, on signal pad from signal Wrens, on crested notepaper from more respectable categories. Letters from Aultbea and Fort William and Dunoon and Scapa and all the other demented places we had landed up in from *Cabbala*.

'Dear S,' wrote my sister, who was eleven, 'I went to a fair last night with the Warrenders. There was a roundabout and frightful bumper cars. The warning went before we left for the fair but we went. As we were waiting for the bus a plane came down very low making funny popping noises. As it came down lower we realised that it was machine-gunning us, so Mrs Warrender screamed and leapt up and down and yelled at the top of her voice "Run!" So we ran. As we ran there was a terrific burst of gunfire and pops and bangs and more machine-gunning. At the fair they all went on those awful chair-o-planes except me because Mum had made me make a solemn vow never to go in one because they are too dangerous.'

While I was reading, Joan was saying, 'Listen to this – I've heard from Margery who was at *Cabbala* – five of them have gone to Macrihanish or Stornoway or somewhere and have only got one double bunk between them, and have only scrubbed floors all the time so far, not signalled at all.'

In the Mess we sat down to porridge and bacon and egg and bread and butter for breakfast; soup, meat with two veg. and tart or steam pudding for lunch; cheese dreams or ham, bread and butter with lemon curd or golden syrup for supper; and tea with everything. It was good, and well cooked, and plentiful, if you weren't a watchkeeper.

On the Mess window seat sat the redoubtable Florence. She was a Leading Hand, and she was Chief Officers' Steward. When she wasn't waiting on the Officers she came into the Mess and gossiped with us. Florence was quite old, maybe even thirty, and had been housekeeper in a stately home in the Midlands. She was the cleanest person I have ever known. Her long, gleaming, brown, straight hair was parted in the exact centre and drawn back into a bun with never a loose hair or a loose hairpin. Her face was polished and shiny. Her collar and shirt were so white it dazzled you to look at them. Her tie was pressed and knotted in a plump knot. Her uniform always kept its original nap and was pressed and creaseless. Her stockings never had holes or ladders. Her shoes were like mirrors. She had a fund of wickedly amusing stories which she told in a deadpan Lancashire accent.

Florence had been at Inverary when a Wren was murdered there. 'Go on, Florence,' we would egg her on callously, 'tell us about the Wren being murdered at Inverary,' and Florence would settle herself on the window seat with a starchy crackle, like an impeccable nannie, and with shameless embroidery tell us again all about it.

Only once did I see Florence's composure crack, and that was when she did the lights-out round at 2300 and found Joan and me in the same bed, trying to stop our teeth chattering by generating a little mutual heat, while the others milled around us in various stages of going to bed. 'Don't *ever* let me see you doing that again,' she hissed in a tone of outraged horror. 'Get into your own beds immediately or I'll get you both dismissed from the Service.' We couldn't think what we had done wrong.

Behind the Mess was the Little Mess, where Chiefie master-minded her campaign against dirt and starvation at Raasay Lodge. It was a coveted retreat, as it had a coal fire with a fender, and a telephone. When boy friends rang up we were allowed to take the calls there, to the accompaniment of ribald comments from anyone who was around. The Little Mess led into the Holy of Holies, the forbidden land, the main hall of the house, with a massive front door used by the Wren Officers, and the Officers' Mess and Common Room, which I never caught a glimpse of. It was the preserve of those splendid well-nourished girls, who never felt the cold in their magnificent greatcoats and smart tricornes. They always reminded me of John Betjeman's 'shining ones, who dwell Safe in the Dorchester Hotel'.

At the back of Raasay Lodge was the galley, a gloomy cavern. We only entered it when we were Duty Orderlies. There was a rota for this event, which entailed spending one evening in the galley when the cooks had finished washing up, making cocoa for the Wrens who were in for the evening and putting hot water bottles in the officers' beds. The 'cocoa' was an abominable confection, which put me off real cocoa for life. A sort of blackish iron brick had to be scraped with a knife to get off a gritty dust, and this was scattered on to an urn of water and stirred while it boiled. It always came out thin, grey, gritty, lukewarm, and with pennies of grease floating on top. On the ships it was made tolerable by being topped up with equal quantities of condensed milk. The officers used to get cold hot water bottles in their beds. It was the only way we could get back at them.

Up from the galley led the Back Stairs – another forbidden land, leading to the cabins of Chiefie and the stewards.

The girl who had scabies was let out of Sick Bay for a day and a night to get married. Her boy friend was on a charge, but they let him out for a day and night too. It was all done in a great hurry, and in fact she never came back. We asked Florence why, and she pursed up her lips and shook her head.

'Did she have a honeymoon then?' I asked wistfully, ever hopeful.

Florence turned away muttering something in an outraged tone.

'*What* did you say?' I asked.

'Pussers pyjamas in a paper bag, that's what I said. That was her trousseau,' and Florence flounced out of the Mess with a toss of her gleaming head.

98

12

Getting on a Boat (Duty)

When we were off duty, we spent more time in the YWCA than anywhere else. It stood on the green between Raasay Lodge and the town, and was a nissen hut. It was warm, bright, chintzy, well equipped, and run by someone called Miss Hindmarsh, who ought to have got a medal at the end of the war for providing all the Services in Oban with the nearest thing to home. There we sat hour after hour, while the gales blew and the rain came down in buckets and outside it was black as ink, and Miss Hindmarsh calmly and cheerfully fed us on hot cheese rolls and coffee. There I sat one autumn evening with Marian, who had come off duty at 1800.

'Did all the convoy come in?' I whispered to her.

'Still stragglers,' she hissed back. 'I think four.'

The Atlantic merchant ship convoys used the anchorage off Lismore as a gathering point before sailing south to the Clyde under escort. Usually they came stealing in and out at night, but if they had had to scatter the stragglers went on arriving at odd hours for a day or so.

Above the buzz of conversation Miss Hindmarsh shouted, ''Phone for you Stephanie – it's urgent.'

I could only think of the First Lieutenant, and a rapid review of all I might have done wrong in the past few hours passed before my eyes.

It was Dave. 'There's a trip for you if you're off duty tonight. They want to get this convoy shifted down to the Clyde as soon as possible, and there are still three stragglers. We're sending a drifter, the *Lord Collingwood*, out to look for them and the skipper wants a signalman who can cope. You've got an hour before she sails – take all the clothes you've got, collect the berthing instructions and an Aldis and battery from Base, and for God's sake don't disgrace me and be seasick.'

An hour later I was picking my way between the bollards on the pier. I had collected my seaman's jersey and two other sweaters from Raasay Lodge, and an oilskin and sou'wester, and had been given an Aldis and battery and three large buff envelopes at Base.

The *Lord Collingwood* was a pilot drifter, to which we signalled daily. The pier was so dark it was difficult to find her, but a seaman was looking out for me and shone a pencil light from a torch for me to cross the gang plank. We cast off and chugged out of Oban bay, past Dunollie light, and round the north coast of Kerrera towards the open sea. Behind us I could just see a glimmer of light from the signal station at Ganavan.

The skipper said, 'Ye can go below lass – the lads are brewing the tea,' but I couldn't waste a moment of the Hebridean night in the wheelhouse, with the little ship starting to rise to the Atlantic waves. It had been comparatively warm in the town, but as soon as we left the land behind it became piercingly cold, colder than I had ever known. The air lined my lungs with ice.

I sipped at a big steaming tin mug of tea topped up with condensed milk, and gulped down hunks of crusty bread and plum jam. The skipper gestured to starboard. 'We're past the south coast of Mull now – yon's Iona,' he said. It was the nearest I ever got to Iona.

About an hour later the mate said, 'There's one!' I picked up the Aldis and made contact. I could make out a cliff ahead slightly blacker than the black of the sea, with the familiar triangle of masthead, port and starboard light. The engine was only just audible. We crept alongside. There was a clank, and a bucket on a long chain descended on the deck. I put in one of the buff envelopes. 'Haul away!' shouted the skipper. 'Okay bud, we'll make our own way in!' a voice shouted back.

The skipper shouted up, 'There are two still missing – have you seen them?'

'The *Hiram J. Doppelganger* is about a mile back, mebbe less,' the shout came back. 'The *Silas X. Vanderburger* had steering trouble – she's further.'

We came up with the *Hiram J. Doppelganger* in about an hour, and repeated the procedure.

It was midnight. I went below to thaw my hands. The cabin smelt fuggily of oil and wet clothes and bread and tea. There were eight double-decker wooden bunks built into the sides towards the bows. Two of the crew were sitting at the table eating. They grinned and pushed more food towards me. I couldn't bear to stay below long in case I missed anything.

100

In the wheelhouse, I began to realise that looking through a telescope and using an Aldis is one thing when the horizon stays steady, but quite another when it is over your head one minute and under your feet the next. It gave me a stab of guilt to remember the times I had cursed the signalmen for their erratic, unreadable signals. At 0200 I said to the skipper, 'I believe I can see her.' He had a look and said, 'You're right, lassie.' I called her up on the swaying Aldis, bracing myself against the side of the wheelhouse, while the *Lord Collingwood* lurched and wallowed through the sea. 'Yes,' I told the skipper, 'it's the *Silas X. Vanderburger.*'

'Ask her if she can make it to the anchorage.'

I did, and reported that her steering was damaged and she needed us to take her right to her berth. We crept up to the side of the third black cliff. I could see flakes of rust as we bumped against the steel plates. The deck overhung us and we moved out a little way so that the third bucket would land on deck and not overshoot into the sea. I put the third buff envelope in the bucket and put my head right back to look up and see if I could see who was pulling it up. My sou'wester fell off and I heard an incredulous voice say, 'God Almighty, it's a girl!' Heads were visible popping up over the side. Another voice said, 'Say, was that you on the lamp? Gee, you're good!' I sketched a wave and then we drew away and started to lead the ship in.

It took until 0500 to get back, up the Firth of Lorne, past the Lady's Rock lighthouse on the tip of Lismore, and over to the southern anchorage. There were enormous black shapes lying still all round us on the water. We crawled past them until we reached a gap.

'This is it,' said the skipper.

Suddenly the most ear-splitting noise I had ever heard rent the air, and miles of rusty anchor chain crashed into the sea beside us. I felt as though every German between Oban and New York must have heard it. Then the night was utterly still except for the puttering of our engine as we headed back into Oban bay.

The sky was just getting light as I walked up Oban front at 0700. Time for a wash and breakfast before walking out to Ganavan to go on watch at 0800.

I thought it was a marvellous war.

One night in December, Rosemary went out in one of the tugs, the *Empire Naiad*, to get a Depot Ship off the rocks on the far side of Mull. She didn't come back the next morning, and Carol had to do a double watch for her. Marian and I took over at lunch time. We could hardly keep our feet as we climbed the cliff, the wind was so strong. The Ensign was tearing itself to tatters and there were white horses right across the bay. We pulled ourselves up the outside ladder with the wind flattening us in gusts against the rail.

It started getting dark at 1400. Steps came clanking up the ladder and there was Dave, looking haggard.

'Strong tea,' he said in a taciturn way, and started chain smoking, biting his nails between puffs.

Marian said chattily, 'Is Rosemary back yet?'

'Do us a favour and belt up,' said Dave. 'Haven't I got enough on my hands with this bloody gale? And by the way, you needn't mention to Blondie that Rosemary isn't back yet.'

We realised Dave hadn't got permission from the Wren Officers to send a Wren out. Our hearts warmed to him for giving us the chance to see a bit of action. We felt like comforting him.

I said, 'But surely the *Naiad* can ride out a gale?'

'It's not the *tug* I'm worried about, it's Rosemary.'

'Oh, Rosemary will be OK Dave, she's *never* seasick.'

'She can bring up all her guts for all I care – I'm not worried about *that*.'

'Then?'

'Oh hell – it's the skipper. I know him.'

'She's awfully strong-minded and capable,' said Marian hopefully after a pause.

'Much good will that do her,' said Dave gloomily. 'I doubt if she'll be back tomorrow – that's probably three nights. They'll have to ride it out – they couldn't get the *Bonaventure* back to Ardrishaig in this. The forecast is worse.'

The next day the other tug, the *Empire Dryad*, set out to try and get Rosemary off, but had to turn back as it was too rough to reach the *Naiad*.

We went on doing Rosemary's watches. We looked at each other but we didn't discuss it.

The fourth day I was doing an extra watch with Carol in the evening. The gale had dropped a bit but it was still very dark. Little Ganavan 'phoned and Bert said, 'Crossing on one.' I picked out a triangle of masthead, port and starboard lights, and flashed it. Back came, 'Rosemary here – request berth for *Empire Naiad*. I'll be with you in an hour for night watch.' I said, 'Go back to Quarters and get some sleep.' She sent the acknowledgement but didn't answer. The tug disappeared into harbour.

An hour later Rosemary stomped up the ladder looking weatherbeaten. 'Hallo toots,' she said with her usual grin.

'How did you get on?' we asked.

'OK,' she said.

'What did you do at night?' tentatively said Carol.

'Barricaded myself in the skipper's cabin while he was on watch. Slept like a top.'

'What was the skipper like?'

'OK toots,' she said laconically.

Next time I went to sea, it was to meet a damaged Canadian corvette, and escort her to the refit base at Dunstaffnage, north of Ganavan. I was on a fishing boat called the *Gracie Ann*. She was like a little Noah's Ark, with the deck sloping steeply up to a point in the bow and stern, and a tiny wheelhouse like an upright shoe box amidships. I reported at 0500 on a very cold February morning. The skipper said, 'Shouldna' be more'n a few hours, lassie – the wee corvette knows the rendezvous and the ETA* and it's a bonnie nicht. Ye'll save us the time if you can tell her where to go and we needna' close with her.'

We went down the Sound of Kerrera, and south to the rendez-vous point near Loch Nell Bay. There was no sign of the corvette but it was getting light by then so there was no danger of missing her. The skipper anchored.

There we sat, on this midget little bath-tub boat. There was a steep sea, and we were pitching up and down from bow to stern and rolling from side to side. I looked up at the matchstick mast which was describing irregular circles on a Payne's grey sky. I looked down at the deck, which sloped pretty steeply even when the boat was at rest, and was now running the gamut of every kind of straight line except the horizontal. I didn't feel very happy inside but I thought I should be able to cope if the corvette came soon.

The skipper said, 'Go below lass for a warm up – the lads have made some tea.' I staggered down the miniature ladder. Below

---

*Expected Time of Arrival

103

was the cabin, like every working ship's cabin, only very small this time. The deck went up to a point at the bow end, there were two wooden berths, one each side of the bows, and a table and bench bolted down. There was the same blackish sweetish tea, and a doorstep of bread and jam and a chunk of fruit cake.

I started to eat, and fixed my eyes on the nearest bunk as an anchor. It went up over my head and circled round to the left and over my right shoulder and came back under my right foot. Suddenly I made a bolt for the ladder and the haven of the side of the boat.

'There, there, lassie,' the skipper said. 'It's being anchored see – it's not like moving along. Why don't you go below and lie on my bunk for a wee while. I'll call ye when I see her.'

For once I accepted the offer. The bunk was cosy and warm, and I pulled a heavy hairy cover, which felt like some sort of skin, up to my chin. I shut my eyes and then I was going round with the boat, not fighting it, and it was all right.

At 0800 the skipper called me. It was getting light and the corvette was just in sight, disappearing and reappearing over the dark grey waves. I hitched my arm round the edge of the wheelhouse and tried to keep the Aldis trained on her, but the beam wavered around. Luckily she had a bright signalman who guessed at what he couldn't make sense of, and we started up and preceded the corvette back north towards Dunstaffnage.

The harbour looked so different coming in from the sea – everything was back to front and seemed a different size. In this looking-glass world, Lady's Rock lighthouse was on the port beam and Kerrera on the starboard. Although there were white horses, it seemed very calm after the heavy seas outside. We got back to Oban harbour at midday. I hoped Dave would never find out that for the only time in my life I had been seasick.

As I walked up the front to Raasay Lodge I realised I had been scratching and scratching for the last two hours, my arms and legs and round the middle and up to my neck. There were huge red bites visible round my wrists. I remembered the lovely cosy skin rug.

Vanessa Class, HMS *Cabbala*, summer 1943

Ganavan Signal Station

Rosemary up the mast

Tuesday May 16, 1

AMERICAN RED CROSS

Dear Stephanie:

I suppose this will come as quite a surprise to you, but I promised to write and I am one who always keeps a promise.

By now you probably think I am a pretty fresh guy because of some of the things I said by Blinker. Maybe you didn't know it but I have been trying for quite some time to think of some excuse to strike up a conversation. I learned from the pilot that there were Wrens in the signal tower, so I says to myself says I " If these girls are as friendly as everyone says they are, maybe they

Jack's letter

would consider cheering up the lonely heart
of an American Sailor?

From the description I received of you
I would say you are very nice. If you would
send me your picture I will assure you that
you would become the "pin-up girl" of the
Matt W. Ransom.

I am making this letter short so it
will not be too boring. I will be very
pleased if I receive an answer from you.
So don't let me down.

An admirer,

Jack.

I'm not sure how you should
address a letter to me in this port,
but you can try sending it on:

Jack Campbell SM3k
S.S. Matt W. Ransom (ship 560)

The road to Oban

V/S Wren Stephanie

Jack Campbell

Rosemary, Joan and Stephanie on Lismore

Dunollie House

The Firth of Lorne

13

On the Town

As I came out of Raasay Lodge, Auld Hamish leaned on his besom, took a deep breath, and said on a wheezing note, 'Are ye awa' agen?'

'Aye,' I replied. I had discovered why the Scots said 'aye' so much. It was the only possible reply to the kind of phraseology they used. So I had taken a leaf out of their books. Anyway, today I was too busy to bother. I had an afternoon off watch and a lot to do in the town.

First I drew my week's pay, £1, which made me feel quite rich. None of us had had jobs which subsidised us through the war and expected us back after, and none of us had parents who could afford to send us money, so we were all living on £1 a week for ever, which probably saved us developing a Trade Union mentality.

Then I went to the NAAFI and traded my weekly chocolate coupon for two bars of chocolate.

To finish with officialdom, I then called in at slops. The Naval Stores was where we exchanged chits for Service clothing and other necessities of life. I had promised to buy a pair of Wren pyjamas for my mother to give my sister for Christmas. I got a nice thick striped meridian pair – that was 3s 11d. My mother's only suggestion for a Christmas present for herself was a comb or a lipstick. I got a beautiful tortoiseshell comb for 3d but it seemed rather little for a Christmas present. They had no lipsticks.

I came out into the shopping street. The swanky shop was Chalmers down the bottom end, where they sold plaid and made kilts. Some shops would take Naval chits for civilian clothes, but Chalmers was too grand. The only thing a Wren could buy there was a tartan tie on a black tie chit – I suppose their Calvinistic consciences would stretch to that. I had already bought a Dress Stewart tie, in soft wool, with a Chalmers label on the back, and it was the apple of my eye. But I couldn't wear it with a Service shirt and I hadn't got a blouse with the right sort of neck. Something would eventually have to be unpicked and dyed and remade.

I went into a newsagent and asked if they had any lipsticks. 'Ye'll no get a lipstick in Oban,' said the elderly lady with scrubbed pale lips, in a self-satisfied way. I was conscious of my lips slashed with Battle Red. She regarded me with distaste.

I went up the road to a chemist. 'No lipsticks delivered for weeks,' he said. My heart warmed to him because he didn't add, 'Don't you know there's a war on?'

I said, 'I suppose you haven't got any rosehip syrup?' He eyed me owlishly. 'Are ye an expectant mother then?'

I didn't know if he was serious but I thought I caught a twinkle in his eye. 'Nine months,' I said, 'and I've got a craving.'

His face split in a leathery grin and he took a bottle from under the counter and pushed it over to me. 'Next week,' he hissed, 'I might have a tin of blackcurrant purée, if ye're under six months old.'

'I'll bring my rattle,' I said.

My mother would have to try and get a lipstick herself- there might be one in Croydon.

Up by the North Pier I passed the Columba Hotel. You could go that way in the day, but after dark that corner was a place to avoid. The Allies were apt to congregate and spring out. Round they flocked one night, in navy tammies with red pompoms – 'Ah, ze leetle Wren, she like ze Free French! She like them vairy much!' 'No, she doesn't,' I said, giving the nearest one a firm push in the chest, 'she can't stand the Free French.'

A bit further up the town my eye was always caught by a large hoarding made of tin, nailed very high to the wall of a building – 'They come as a boon and a blessing to men, the Pickwick, the Owl and the Waverley Pen.' I never had the faintest idea what it meant. I believe it was an advertisement. The three greatest blessings to women, if they had been invented then, would have been Kleenex, Tampax, and plastic bags.

I cut one street inland to look in the window of the Gem Box. That was where the money went. A whole mouth-watering window of silver, Galleys of Lorne, necklaces, brooches, bracelets. At the moment I was faint with desire for Robert Bruce's battleaxe in silver, one inch long, with a little cornelian in the handle. But it was 5s and I would have to save up for it. It would look smashing on the Dress Stewart tie. Or was that a clash of clans?

I went into the little draper which took our chits for vests and knickers and handkerchiefs and sold us skirts and blouses in exchange. At any new Base to which you were drafted, the first question was, 'Which shops do chit-wangles?' A very efficient grape-vine covered every shop in the British Isles. We always traded the handkerchief chits, because we made handkerchiefs out of old parachutes. I was busy at the moment embroidering initials on a batch for Christmas presents. As Kleenex hadn't been invented, everybody had to have handkerchiefs.

The draper had a yellow blouse which might take a tie, but it would clash with my only civilian skirt which was pink and my only pair of civilian shoes, a very old suede pair dyed green. I thought I might look like a firework. Just as well: I couldn't afford it this week.

As I passed the fleahouse, a wave of lysol engulfed me. They were showing *Once on a Honeymoon*. Further up was the bughouse, with *Something to Sing About*. I had seen them both. There weren't any other cinemas. Seats were 9d, with one free night a week for Forces.

At the top of a very respectable block of flats lived a very respectable elderly couple whom I visited occasionally on a rather vague introduction at third remove from someone at home. It crossed my mind to look in, in case they were having tea. But I had a bad conscience about them – last time I went there they warned me in dire tones about the awful goings on at the weekly Petty Officers' Dance at one of the hotels, and said they were sure my mother wouldn't like me to go anywhere like that. I agreed in shocked tones, with a ticket for the next PO's Dance burning a hole in my pocket.

What really annoyed me was that they were quite right. The sailors at dances were always drunk, but at that dance they were drunk to the point of vomiting all over the floor and sitting in it singing. So I went back to Quarters after half an hour.

I had got to the Argyllshire canteen and suddenly I was absolutely starving. I tried to remember when I last ate. Four sardine sandwiches at 0300. Too late back for breakfast. Half a cup of cold rice pudding smuggled up to the cabin in a brown paper bag at 1400.

The Argyllshire was not so popular as the YWCA. It was

gloomier and more Scottish. It was presided over by one of the formidable ladies of Oban. She wore black with a black velvet ribbon round her throat, a black velvet hat, and gloves Sometimes I helped to wash up in the Argyllshire. I liked to hear the kind of lives the charity ladies led. I respected them deeply. I m sure they worked harder than anybody. They said they didn't really like Service people helping, but they didn't mind me because I was a Nice Girl and there wouldn't be any Funny Business

I said 'Hallo' to the back view of a large woman who was frenziedly dashing plates through a bowl of water and stacking them on a draining board. She was wearing a torn black overall and an ancient green felt hat, her stockings were wrinkled and her shoes covered with mud. 'Hallo my dear, sorry no time to turn round,' she shouted. She was Mrs Ballantyne, who was very rich and had a chauffeur and a secretary. She told me once that since the war started she had never had time to do any mending and all her clothes were held together with safety pins. 'When I get into bed at night, the room is just littered with safety pins,' she said. As took my cup of tea over to a table she leaned on the sink for a moment and said, 'The only thing I want, when the war is over, is a day, just one day, in bed.'

The Melancholy Marine came over to my table. I think he lived in the Argyllshire canteen – we never saw him anywhere else. He had bristling brows and deeply furrowed cheeks. He looked at me for a long time and then said dubiously, was I the sort of girl who liked dances and cinemas and town life. 'Oh no,' I breathed hopefully. There are only two worth while things in Oban,' he said, 'golf and fishing. Every Saturday I catch the bus out to a splendid trout stream and have lunch in the hotel near. I stay in the river until it's dark. You and your friends could come too if you like.'

I thanked him profusely.

Apart from the YWCA, the only other canteen was the TOFAC – the Flying Angel Club – run by the Missions to Seamen. We didn't go there because it was so bleak- there was only a battered billiard table. It seemed sadly hampered by religion

I passed the Alexandra – the Oban equivalent of the Dorchester – where the Naval Officers lived in splendour. Then the Park, where the RAF lived, and where the RAF Chaplain held gramophone recitals and played 'Fingal's Cave' and 'Enigma Variations'. We liked going there because it was warm.

Up by the Park Hotel one night, Joan and I met the Russians. There was a Russian sub-chaser in for the night. Russians to me meant *Prince Igor* and *Scheherazade* and *Petrushka* and *Firebird*. Now here were three of them, with flat caps and flattish faces and rather pointed teeth and curious short full jackets.

We tried 'Tovarich,' and they grinned. No English. We took them to the YWCA. They were our gallant allies and we had to look after them. Cinema? we said. We took them to the fleahouse – they probably had fleas already, Russian fleas. They couldn't understand a word but it didn't matter. Huge moony faces dripping with tears swam out at us. The dialogue was something like, 'Can you understand now Madeleine why it is that I have loved you all these years and never spoken of my love?' 'Oh Alaric, my dearest, but I have known always that you loved me, we loved each other before the dawn of time.' The Russians munched at cornets with their feral teeth and looked impassive and Mongolian.

When we came out it was dark and raining. We made signs that we had to be back by 2000. Suddenly we were all arm in arm and they were singing in time to our tramping feet. The 'Volga Boatmen'? No. We had some difficulty in identifying the words and the tune, but suddenly we were with them. 'Lay that pistol *down* babe, lay that pistol *down*, pistol-packin' Momma, lay that pistol *down!*'

Up the rainswept Oban front we tramped, arm in arm, yelling it louder and louder, enough to shake those po-faced houses down; 'Lay that pistol *down* babe, lay that pistol *down* – pistol-packin Momma, lay that pistol *down!*' Their huge jovial voices rang out.

Outside Raasay Lodge they swept off their caps, bowed over our hands, clicked their heels, and were off.

When I got up to the YWCA I decided to stoke up for the evening with a coffee and a cheese roll, even though that would run me down to 15s 2d. I shared a table with three RAF Corporals.

'Tell us,' they said, 'are you the sort of girl who likes country walks and fishing and golf?'

'Good grief, no,' I said.

'Yippee!' they said. 'We've just arrived, and we're going to paint Oban red and organise dances galore!'

'Oh good-oh!' I said. But I never saw them again.

When I got back to Raasay Lodge, Joan met me. 'Guess what,' she said.

'You've got a draft south.'

'No. We've each got a tomato for tea!' I hadn't seen one for about six months. It made my day.

14

Leave

I spent the first quarter of my 21st birthday in Euston Station. After three months' hard labour, including a period when all leave was cancelled, the iron grip of the Hebrides loosened, a tiny gap in the ring of mountains got minutely wider each day, and we were gradually filtered out one by one. The survivors did double watches.

The day before my birthday, which was in the middle of the winter, I set the alarm for 0500 and crept out of the silent Raasay Lodge, into a pitch black rainy night, and down the windswept front to the Station, for the 0600 train. Joan had helped me carry my case down the night before. My father had promised to meet me at Euston at 2100, but by Stirling we were already late and as the train meandered on through Carlisle, down to Crewe, we stopped again and again while goods trains clanked by on their priority journeys. There was no heat in the train, no water, and of course no food. Every time it stopped at a station someone made a foray for buns and tea.

We got to Watford at 2300 and took another hour to get to Euston. I could see searchlights. I spent the last half hour making up my face, by the light of one dimmed bulb, for the lightning dash home, trying to plaster over the cracks round my eyes with the latest pancake. The sailor opposite watched me in a sort of frozen torpor. 'I'm awfully sorry,' I said. 'Please don't apologise,' he said, 'it's been quite fascinating.'

My father had been waiting four hours, having gone home to supper after a day's work in London, and come back again – an hour and half's journey each way. It wasn't difficult – suburban trains and buses ran frequently and always on time. He said, 'I'm afraid we've missed the last train – we'll have to stay here till the morning.'

I said, 'I'm twenty-one.'

He said, 'Mm.' Neither of us could indulge in the luxury of ordinary feelings about such an event. This was war time.

111

We sat on benches in the waiting room and got the first tube to Victoria at 0600. Clattering down through the suburbs, I could see that there were fresh holes all over London. We got home to breakfast. I looked at my parents and my sister across the table. I thought they looked thinner and older, and I looked younger and much, much fatter. I didn't quite fit into the jigsaw any more.

'The Austins' had a direct hit last week,' my Mother said emotionlessly. She didn't say any more, and I didn't ask. A direct hit meant that the house no longer existed, and nobody had survived. I would miss them when I had time to think about it, but not yet. For now, it was pushed into the back of my mind, behind Ganavan.

My father's daily plod to the office, or what was left of it, my sister's dancing classes, my Mother's daily battle to feed the family, went the same way. Even the cat looked at me cautiously, sensing tension.

We would never be the same close-knit group again. We were adjusting to a different world, in different ways, and the adjustment was beyond me. Ganavan had become my home, and the Ganavan Wrens my closest relations.

After breakfast, my father got a bus and a train back to the City, where his office was.

My mother said, 'I've got tickets for the matinee at the New – Comus, Promenade and Job. Helpmann and Fonteyn. Lunch at the Trocadero, I thought.' I had never been to the Trocadero before. So we went up to town.

When we came back the Air Raid siren sounded. The guns started to boom. We put up the blackout curtains and went to bed.

I only got to the ballet in London once more before the end of the war, on a 48-hour leave with Joan. We saw Carnaval, Nocturne and Spider's Banquet at the New. We wore civvies, and in the interval we put on our snootiest accents and said to each other, 'Oh my deah, the whole place is seething with those ghastly Service women, so frumpish in uniform, I don't know how they can.' A dowager-like woman in front of us turned round and glared. 'Wait for the white feather,' hissed Joan.

On my 21st birthday leave I went back to the office where I'd worked. 'You do look well,' my friends said accusingly. 'How lucky you are – of course you get all the best food we can't get, and all those marvellous Service dances.' I thought they must have been seeing too many wartime films.

After three days I was beginning to wonder what was going on in Oban. After a week I felt as if I had been away for a year.

I arrived back in Oban in the middle of one of the gales. This was not just a question of strong wind. It was impossible to stand upright without holding on to something. Hunks of seaweed came hurtling over the front and across the road, full grown trees went bowling along like hoops, you had to yell to make yourself heard.

As I dragged myself, bent double, from bush to bush up the front path of Raasay Lodge I passed Auld Hamish, sheltering in the lee of the porch, sharpening a scythe. 'Cauld,' he quaked. 'Aye,' I said.

Inside the wind was shaking the stone house to its foundations The lights were out, because the wind was blowing the blackout curtains vertically into the rooms through the closed windows.

Thank goodness you're back,' said Carol. 'Do you mind doing night watch to relieve Rosemary? She did all last night and she's still there now.'

I dumped my case on my bed and launched myself on to the Ganavan road. Dunollie point was a slight windbreak at first. Round the corner the gale hit me and I clawed from tree to tree, while branches clashed overhead and the foam blew up from the shore. There were white horses galloping in and not a ship to be seen.

Just before the path up to the cliff a smallish tree was lying across the road, a few shrivelled-looking leaves still clinging to what had been its top, and its earthy roots sticking up in the sky. I climbed over it and up to the Signal Station where the wind was shrieking like banshees round the mast.

There was a sulky looking sailor in a crash helmet sitting by the stove reading the *Daily Mirror*. He didn't look up.

'Who's he?' I yelled to Rosemary. 'Despatch rider,' she mouthed back. ''Phone lines are all down.'

At that moment we both saw a light flashing, near in. Rosemary shouted, 'They couldn't get through with the Aldis batteries – you'll have to use the ten-inch. This afternoon the electricity was off – we had to do semaphore from the roof.' Thank goodness it was too dark for that now.

I dragged on the oilskin coat and a sou'wester, but I couldn't get out of the door against the wind. I put my lips to Rosemary's ear and bellowed, 'Rope! Tie me on!'

We clung to each other, hooked our arms round the wire of the balustrade, and inched our way along the balcony to the ten-inch. Rosemary wound the rope round me and the metal frame. The wind clamped me on to the back of the lamp. As I pushed down the shutter the steady beam shone comfortingly out.

'Patrol boat,' said the answering light, weaving crazily around. 'They want help in Port Appin. Am going to try and get through. Inform Base.'

Rosemary managed to untie me and we crawled back. The Despatch Rider was still reading the *Daily Mirror*.

'You'll have to go to Base,' I shouted, not without relish. 'There's a signal they must have.'

When he had disappeared I yelled to Rosemary, 'I didn't tell him there's a tree down on the road.'

After leave and the gales, there were months of unremitting winter to get through. I was on watch with Catharine, who had been rich before she joined up, and had never had to have a job. She was a plump, creamy girl, with brown curly hair and a cosy bosom. She used to tell me about her boarding school, and the clothes she bought with an allowance from her father, and her horse, and the parties she went to.

One night, she said, 'I shall go out of my tiny mind soon if I don't get out of this dump. I have decided that we shall get two nights' SOP and go to Edinburgh.'

'Why Edinburgh?' I said.

'Because, my child, there is Culture in Edinburgh. And, which is much more to the point, there are Polish Officers, hundreds of them so I'm told, based in the Caledonian Hotel.'

Thinking of post-war invitations to spend the summer in Catharine's little schloss outside Cracow, I agreed.

'I shall write to the hotels and select one suitable to our social status,' she said. And as many a true word is spoken in jest, she found that the hotels were all full, and we ended up in the YWCA. The Warden wrote that she would keep 'two nice beds' for us. Catharine sniffed.

We left Oban at midday on Friday, but the train was very late and didn't get to Edinburgh until 2315. It had started to snow the day before – white and glittery in Oban, but black and slushy in Edinburgh.

The Warden seemed peeved to see us and said there was nothing to eat or drink at that hour. We hadn't had anything since lunch and were shaking with cold and hunger. She showed us into a very small bleak room with two iron beds and one blanket on each; convoys were thundering by outside and rattling the windows. We piled all our clothes on the beds, topped with great-coats, and huddled under them all night unable to sleep Snow seeped in through gaps in the sash.

Catharine said as we were dragging our damp stockings over our icy feet in the morning, 'We used to go to Daddy's villa near Nice in the summer for a month or two, the sailing was heavenly.'

When we went out I realised that Edinburgh was black. All the buildings, the streets, the cobbles, the trams, the urchins begging in the gutters, even the snow sleeting down, which had started white but turned black before it reached the sky above Edinburgh.

We went round the shops, and the bit of the Castle which hadn't been turned into a hospital. We saw the War Memorial and the National Gallery. In the evening, a friend of Catharine's gave us dress circle tickets for the new Eric Linklater play. 'It's quite interesting seeing a show from the auditorium', she said. 'In London we always have a box.'

On Sunday we went to the Forth Bridge and over in the ferry. It was snowing black snow so hard that we couldn't see the Bridge. We had lunch at the inn there, of scotch broth, roast beef, Yorkshire pudding, apple tart and cider. I had to admit it was the first real food I'd had since I was home on leave. Dutifully we plodded round Holyrood, which was arctic. The gardens were under water.

We were splashed up to the knees with black slush and our faces and hands were mauve. We went back to the YWCA to clean up. I could see that Catharine had the light of battle in her eyes, by the way she made up her face and scooped her hair into a tidy brown roll well clear of her collar. Through the black portals of the Caledonian Hotel she dragged me with lips set. 'Dinner for two,' she said, in the ringing voice which had fetched them up from the depths of the Ritz. We had soup, and fish, and fruit flan.

Afterwards came the apotheosis. We sat in the lounge eking out our cups of coffee, too stunned by the price to speak – they cost 9d each. 'How dare they,' said Catharine, with a spot of colour on each cheek. 'Daddy would never stand for it.'

Down the main staircase like a film set came the Polish Officers, resplendent in their uniforms, tall, suave, sophisticated, with piercing blue eyes. They were stunning. So were the girls they were escorting – blonde, willowy, with remote expressions and racehorse legs, slinky silk dresses and short fur jackets, and egg-size rings on their engagement fingers. They sauntered through, and the Commissionaire called up taxis for them.

I could see that we might as well take our clumping black boots and sweaty serge back to Bonnie Oban Bay.

'It's no good,' I said to Catharine. 'Your hair's the wrong colour.' She gave me a furious look and then we both dissolved into giggles.

We got the 0655 back to Oban on Monday morning, in the black dark. By midday when we went past Loch Awe the sun was hot through the train window, the sky was blue, and normal white snow was lying in the hollows of the bumpy ground. It looked like Switzerland.

I got a lift up to Raasay Lodge with a transport driver. 'Weren't you lucky, he said, 'hot and sunny all the weekend.'

15

Dunollie

After all the excitement, I was bored. I had been on night watch the night before with Win, who bored me to tears and had a Liverpool accent. Instead of capping my more outrageous fancies, she killed them stone dead with either, 'Eee, you are awful!' or 'Eee you are a scream, you ought to write a book!'

Win was still asleep in the cabin and snoring like thunder, so I got up at 1400 for once and put on a clean shirt and a skirt and polished my shoes on the bedspread. I had an idea. I took myself two doors up the road from Raasay Lodge to a similar pile which had a Red Cross board in the front garden and a small notice in one of the bay windows, 'Wanted – a volunteer on Tuesday afternoons 2-4.'

I was ushered into a large front room, sketchily furnished, with woollen garments hung like tapestries from the picture rail all round. Three plump middle-aged ladies were bustling round a small elderly person who was seated in an armchair with a file of papers on her lap. Having worked in the office of the Matron of a London teaching hospital through the blitz, I was immediately able to recognise the presence of ultimate Authority, tempered with charity.

'This,' respectfully said the lady who had brought me in, 'is The Wren. A volunteer.' And to me, 'This is Mrs MacDougall.'

Mrs MacDougall of MacDougall, wife of Colonel MacDougall, head of the clan MacDougall, mistress of Dunollie Castle and Dunollie House, owner of all Ganavan including the hill on which the Signal Station stood.

In a crisp well-bred voice she said, 'I'm very grateful for your offer of help. Now what I really want is someone who can do some typing. I suppose it's too much to hope that you're a Writer?' Her eyes twinkled.

I said, 'V/S – but I can type.' Somehow I knew I didn't have to explain visual signaller. I found out later that her daughter was a Wren.

'Good,' she said. 'And presumably you could use a brand new Imperial?'

In five minutes I was typing away at the table on the best machine I'd ever used, lists of supplies, letters to Branches, accounts – just like the bad old days before I'd joined the Navy. I couldn't quite overcome a slight sense of nostalgia at so much decisiveness and efficiency.

Behind me a faint murmur continued: 'How many bales did you send to Glasgow?' 'I do wish Mrs MacGregor would learn how to cut out pyjamas.' 'Isn't this a perfectly beautiful pair of bed-socks Mrs Ballantyne?' 'How many ounces will you be requiring Mrs MacLachlan?' 'How would you like to try a balaclava this time Mrs MacGarrie?'

Someone said, 'Will you have tea?' and indicated a pale green china cup with the sort of handle you get your finger caught in, in a saucer, with a silver spoon. Someone else said, 'Do have some bread and butter,' and a plate appeared at my elbow, supporting wafer-thin currant bread and butter, and a silver dish of little biscuits. Some vestigial control from the distant past enabled me not to hug the cup and drain the tea at a gulp and snatch the contents of the plate to cram into my mouth shouting while I ate. My limbs seemed large and uncoordinated, swiping biscuits on the floor and knocking bales of jerseys over with my feet.

Mrs MacDougall came and perched on the table. Her tweeds were impeccable – thick, a heathery colour, and just slightly shabby, her voice brisk.

'Do you work at the PSS or in the Station Hotel?' she said.

I said, 'Ganavan.'

Her face lit up. 'I'm so glad,' she said, 'I like to think of Wrens there.' I felt like blushing.

'You know,' she said, 'when the first eight sailors came to Ganavan the Navy billeted them on Dunollie to save them having to cycle right back into town between watches.'

This was news to me. 'What were they like?' I said

A faint shadow of disdain crossed her face. 'Very untidy,' she said. 'When they went I had to pull one of the mattresses into the garden and burn it.' (I presumed this was a euphemism for 'I asked the under footman to …')

118

I said, 'We've still got the blankets the men had on night watch. They've never been washed.'

Mrs MacDougall set her lips and said imperiously, 'A Complaint should have Been Made.'

If only, I thought, she'd been a Wren Officer.

She continued to look at me speculatively, and then said, 'Have you ever used an Oliver typewriter?' I said, 'Yes.'

'Someone has given me one and I can't make it work. I would like you to come up to Dunollie and look at it for me.'

I tried to breathe deeply and keep calm, pulling my cuffs down hard to cover the flea bites on my wrists. 'Thank you, I should like to,' I said.

'Good,' she said. 'Then perhaps you will come to tea with me next Sunday; 4.0pm.'

It was a Royal Command, not an invitation.

In the hall, as I was going out one of the ladies from the back of the room put her hand on my arm and bared her lips in a thin smile. 'Ye'll be awa' to the big hoose then Sunday?' she said. 'I might, if I'm not on duty,' I said, thinking that I would desert if necessary to get there.

I strolled back to Raasay Lodge, humming to myself.

'Where are you going?' said Joan on Sunday.

'To tea at Dunollie.'

'With Colonel and Mrs MacDougall I suppose.'

'Actually, yes.'

'Very funny,' said Joan.

I had never seen Dunollie House before. It lay in a hollow, behind the ruined tower on the mound of the keep, which was all that was left of the original castle. I had passed the wide gate at the top of the town, marked 'Dunollie', hundreds of times. This time, at 1555, I could go through it and up a winding overgrown drive. There were no gardeners left, and no cultivated garden, but the house looked at home in a setting of bushes and trees gone wild, with the keep sheltering it from the sea and the hills rising in a bowl behind. The colours were all brownish, the stone of the house weathered to the earth so that it seemed to have risen out of the stony ground. It was an uncompromisingly angular building, but large enough to take it, with two main storeys of narrow oblong windows and a row of gabled windows in the roof. A wing

119

was set out at right angles at the back, and what looked like an older wing, ivy covered and with two storeys and a much lower roof, ran out at right angles from the front. A large ugly porch had been added. It was enormous compared with the other houses I had seen in Oban but, unlike them, well proportioned and graceful in spite of its bulk and squareness.

Colonel MacDougall answered the door and led me through a square flagstoned hall, with a staircase running up round it to an upper gallery, and tattered banners hanging dimly from above. The drawing room was a long low room in what I imagined was the older part of the house.

The RAF Chaplain was there – a man of piercing purity, with whom even I failed to imagine myself in romantic situations. I knew him slightly from the gramophone concerts he arranged in the Park Hotel, where the RAF Officers lived. There were several other people I didn't know – mercifully no Wren Officers. I thought there were no other Service people at all, until a man in a suit was introduced as a Brigadier.

Mrs MacDougall said, 'This is Stephanie, who is helping me at the Red Cross. Now I know we mustn't ask you about your work, my dear, although we'd all love to – you know, my husband and I can just see the Signal Station from our bedroom window, and sometimes when we are awake in the night we see the lamps flashing and we think how cold you must be, and how long the night must seem.' I realised that she had more idea than most people in the Base about both the romance and the practicality of signalling. 'Now we're all going to talk about different things from the war – music, and books, and travel, and how life will include all those things again one day.' And we did, though at one time I realised that Mrs MacDougall was carrying on a soft conversation with the Brigadier during which he seemed to be asking her advice about military strategy – I didn't doubt that she could give it competently.

A little maid wheeled in a trolley of tea and arranged plates on a cakestand. She reappeared later to remove them and then whispered to Mrs MacDougall, 'Is it all right if I go home now, madam?'

'Yes, of course, dear, it's a long walk and getting dark.' She caught my eye and said, 'She's the only one left now.'

'Do you mean you and the Colonel are here all alone at night?' I said, thinking that the terrors of Ganavan at night would pale beside a whole Dunollie full of ghosts.

'Yes,' she said, 'and you know last night my last hot water bottle leaked and the mattress was soaked and I had to drag it down to the kitchen and get another one off the bed in the guest wing.' She seemed unlucky with mattresses. 'All alone?' I said, looking at her small aristocratic bones and lined face. 'Oh yes,' she said, 'I didn't want to wake the Colonel, he sleeps so badly.'

At the Red Cross next week, one of the other helpers started to put me in the picture in a sibilant whisper. 'Aye, they're a great family – just her and the Colonel left at home – knows as much as anybody in Oban about the war – three daughters – the eldest has the hereditary title of Maid of Lorne.'

Later I met other relatives at Dunollie. One week there was someone in a fur coat wearing very beautiful rings, introduced as Lady Malcolm. The conversation was above my head, as it often was, but it didn't seem to matter. I relaxed, feeling the long shabby room with pale worn rugs and silver framed photographs as the perfect foil for the gentle, humorous, yet so penetratingly erudite remarks being exchanged around me.

When it was time for me to go, Lady Malcolm sprang to her feet and said imperiously, 'Wait five minutes and I will take you back in my taxi.'

In the taxi, she said confidentially, 'I *must* be back by six o'clock because my gel gives me a good high tea before she goes home.' I could appreciate the point. One got polite afternoon tea at Dunollie, which was totally appropriate. Dunollie fed the brain, the heart, the mind, not the stomach, and to my surprise I had discovered that I would put my stomach in second place any day to get to Dunollie.

As the taxi drew up outside Raasay Lodge, she turned to me and said impulsively, 'Isn't it splendid about my nephew commanding the Eighth Army?' As a conversational gambit I found it unanswerable. I smiled weakly and got out of the taxi, then seeing some Wren Officers standing in the front drive I turned back and said in ringing tones, 'Goodbye, Lady Malcolm!'

By the time Sunday tea was a regular event and I was invited to dinner at Dunollie, I could no longer conceal my artistocratic

121

metamorphosis from the others. They were very charitable about it, considering, only making a few cracks about Snooty Steff.

'What will you have for dinner,' said Rosemary, 'grouse?'

'Haggis?' said Marian.

'Cock-a-leekie soup?' said Carol.

Joan said, 'I bet you only get boiled eggs.'

The dining room at Dunollie was magnificent – sombre and panelled, with a huge empty fireplace, and ancestors peering out of blackened paint on the walls. An ancient refectory table ran down its length, bearing silver candlesticks and silver salt cellars.

There were ten of us. The door swung open and in came Colonel MacDougall bearing a silver tray. On it were ten silver egg cups, each containing a brown speckled egg. They were delicious. 'Laid today,' said Mrs MacDougall. It didn't matter- we were discussing 'The Waste Land' and then we went on to *The Magic Flute*.

When I got back Joan said, 'Well, what did you have?'

'I'm not telling,' I said. 'You'd be jealous.'

16

Out of Town

As the year wore on and the weather improved, I went further afield. McCaig's tower was more up from town than out. It was a stiff climb at the back of Oban, and gave a good view across the bay. I suppose more than anything it resembled a bombed-out Albert Hall. Round its vast circumference was a roofless wall with window embrasures and a stony circular space in the middle. Its only advantage was that, not surprisingly, there was never anybody there. I used to plod up there every week to read the new copy of *Punch*, which in those days was funny rather than clever. Sometimes I wrote poems there, but because of the gothic gloom they always turned out rather turgid, like:

> The Hebridean twilight sought in vain
> One time, to lull me from my loneliness;
> A wanton, in abandon she has lain
> Entwined within the silken sea's caress.
> But yet my sad heart heeded not her wiles,
> Whose pledge was sealed in a southern city;
> Dearer by far its charms than all Argyll's,
> You walked its streets with me and taught me pity.

I thought 'wiles' and 'Argyll's' was rather clever.

Further out and up was the Glencruitten walk, by the golf course. This was really more of a snogging walk, but I seemed to draw the sloggers rather than the snoggers. Here for a time I slogged along at the side of an RAF Sergeant called Ted, while he explained to me how wireless sets worked. I didn't have to answer so I tried to assimilate that enormous expanse of sheer scenery at the top of Oban, with miles and miles of bumpy green hillocks crowned by thickets of conifers, and further miles and miles of bumpy mountains, all between me and home and where the real war was going on. Claustrophobia rose in me like nausea, while Ted babbled of kilowatts.

Past Connel, a long way past, you came to Taynuilt. There was nothing there but a trout stream. It was very clear and cold, with a pebbly bottom, and I spent an afternoon there wading about in wellingtons with an RAF Corporal called Steve, scooping up the beautiful water to taste. 'Come on, Steffoldgirl,' he kept saying, 'let's hike on over that moor in the distance.' But he had picked the wrong Wren.

The road and the railway over the top of the hills above Oban went to Connel Ferry, about five miles away. There wasn't a ferry, but there was a very narrow suspension bridge, a quarter of a mile long, which carried the single track road and the single track railway over Loch Etive to Benderloch. When a train was due the road was closed to traffic and pedestrians, by level crossing gates at either end. If a car came along when you were walking over, you had to get up on the railway line to avoid being run over. The bridge was so long that it swayed slightly, and I found when I tried to walk straight across it that I made a weaving course from side to side. It was worth walking out to Connel to have tea at the Falls of Lora Hotel, where they gave you a slop basin. But the bridge came into its own when we went to a dance at the RAF camp on the other side.

The RAF used occasionally to send a transport into Oban to collect Wrens for a dance. The wheels of the transport were too wide apart to fit on the road, so the driver used to manoeuvre the nearside wheels onto the wall overlooking a sheer drop into Loch Etive far below, and the farside wheels onto the edge of the railway the other side. We were told to sit absolutely still and not speak in case we distracted the driver. This hair-raising progress was of course carried out in pitch darkness.

Over the other side, people screamed with relief and flooded into the nearest hut, which was decorated with dingy, tattered bunting. At the far end a three-piece band (piano, drums and sax) was playing. The lyrics were, like almost all the lyrics, maudlin and banal to the extreme.

Until you fall in love a love-song's just another tune
A lover's moon in June, is just another moon;
Until you fall in love, the nights all seem to be the same,
There is no lover's lane, for you.

What was more to the point, like so many of the tunes it was a slow foxtrot, which nobody could do. The RAF did some solo jitterbugging and we sat round the side.

We had spent hours getting ready and were arrayed in clean white shirts and starched collars, pressed ties and tiddley suits. We sat in serried rows, our clumping black shoes and thick black stockings sticking hopelessly out in front of us, our sensible hair rolled off our collars, our faces, scrubbed and weatherbeaten, lightly powdered with Tokalon, looking wholesome and dull and, like Stevie Smith's schoolgirl on the train, '*si peu séduisante*'. We couldn't help being nice girls.

But when love comes to find you, you're in a world apart,
Leave loneliness behind you, and heaven's in your heart;
You'll never hear the blue bird singing in the sky above,
You'll never know that thrill, Until you fall in love.

The RAF were all drinking beer. They never got vomiting drunk, like the sailors.

'He holds her in his arms, would you, would you,' bleated the singer. It was a waltz. A few of us got to our feet and paired off together, one dancing man.

He tells her of her charms, would you, would you,
They met as you and I, and they were only friends,
But before my story ends
He'll kiss her with a sigh, would you, would you,
If the girl were I, would you, would you,
And would you dare to say, let's do the same as they,
I would, would you?

Joan and I finished with a spin, looking at each other with loathing. Suddenly one of the RAF let out a screech and they all flooded out of the door. 'Listen,' said Joan, 'it's the Civvy Transport.' We could hear another engine grinding over the suspension bridge.

However far in the wilds, however remote and uninhabited the area, up they rolled, the Civvies, with Betty Grable and Hedy Lamarr and Ava Gardner and Lana Turner hairstyles, piled up

125

curls in front and long at the back, shiny, tight, bright-coloured, faintly grubby dresses which shot up their thighs as the airmen lifted them over the tailboard, scarlet Cupid's bows, navy blue eye shadow, padded shoulders, sheer stockings with black clocks, high heels. They were a Rentacutie mob, and the airmen just loved them.

Suddenly the hut was jammed with jostling bodies, Air Force blue pressed close to puce satin and turquoise crepe. Round they went, their faces blank, their jaws rhythmically chewing, the bright skirts swirling up to show suspenders and panties. The smell of dust came up from the splintered floor and mingled with the smell of sweat and Californian Poppy. The high-up windows were draped with blackout curtain, the walls were covered with posters about Careless Talk Costs Lives. A trestle table across one corner was draped with a grey, frayed Union Jack, on which stood bottles of beer and lemonade and plates of buns.

'Boom boom boom' went the band. 'I can see you and I, as we were in days gone by,' moaned the singer, a skinny woman with dyed hair and a sad bosom, wearing a long pink satin dress with a too tight skirt, 'when the mighty organ played O Promise Me;

I was yours, you were mine, it was apple-blossom time,
When the mighty organ played O Promise Me.
The day I placed the ring upon your finger
Will forever linger, in my memoree.
Though the years fade away, You're as sweet as yesterday,
When the mighty organ played O Promise Me.

Still we sat along the sides of the hut, on our bentwood chairs, pretending we didn't care, and sipping lemonade. At half time there was a Palais Glide which everyone could join in, but we had lost heart by then. The band had a break and the hall miraculously emptied in two minutes of airmen and civvies. There were squeals from outside.

The band drank beer, and then struck up one of the silly songs.

Mairzy doats and dozy toats and little lambzy tivy
And a kiddly tivy too, wouldn't you?

to which we sang

126

Motor boats and Carley floats and little rubber dinghies
And I'll paddle my own canoe, wouldn't you?

In they all came again and on we sat. I shut my eyes and thought about Fred Astaire and ballrooms and dinner dances and evening dresses, which I'd never seen except on the silver screen.

About 2200 they did the Hokey Cokey, and then a sea of forage caps and shiny curls piled into transports outside, with much squealing and pinching going over the tailboard, and glimpses of lacy panties, and shot off somewhere. We were lucky if they left behind an elderly wall-eyed driver to take us back home.

When we came out it was cool and quiet and dark. I imagined the cool, quiet, dark sea at Ganavan, the feel of the Aldis in my hand, the pencil of light answering. I wished I'd been on duty. The others crouched round me in the back of the transport, their faces glimmering in the faint light from the dashboard, with sad fixed smiles and faraway eyes. I thought that in some ways we were brave, and I wondered if any of us would ever be happy.

17

Jeannie

For once I got a lift back to Raasay Lodge in a naval transport, which stopped for me. 'Ye've got a new Wren,' said the driver. He winked at his mate. 'I've just brought her from the station.'
'What's she like?'
'Bonnie.'
'Aye,' said his mate caustically, 'She's bonnie all reet. Frae Glasgae. Name of Jeannie.'
She was sitting on Win's recently vacated bed. What a change from Win's homespun potato-face. Jeannie had a tip-tilted nose, even white teeth, and blonde hair which I could see was naturally curly. I could see too that she was the sort of girl who, if left at the bottom of the cliff in a deserted landscape with two Aldis batteries, would appear sunny and empty-handed at the Signal Station, saying deprecatingly, 'This sweet boy just happened to be passing,' and a sailor with an expression of dog-like devotion would dump the batteries down in front of her.
Jeannie was wearing a neat diamond ring. 'Are you engaged then?' I asked. 'Och aye,' she said, looking slantingly up at me with eyelashes fluttering.
'What's his name?'
'Och, he's Hairy.'
'Well, yes, I know, they usually are – oh I see what you mean.'
When she had settled in, Hairy came to stay in the town for a week. It was suddenly summer, and when she was off duty they bolted off together to find a patch of long grass out of range of the Signal Station telescope. When she was on duty he waited at the foot of the cliff with his eyes riveted on the Signal Station. Dave came up specially and unscrewed the big telescope to try and locate them – he said, a girl with boobs like that, he couldn't bear to miss it. I wouldn't let Hairy come up the cliff; he was a civilian, something to do with shipbuilding on the Clyde, and rules were very strict about allowing anyone near the Signal Station.
Jeannie became very anxious to make expeditions down the

cliff for more coal, which the sailors had left lying beside the road. Every time she went plunging down through the gorse bushes, scattering sheep, she took him a cup of tea. When she panted back she seized the telescope and swivelled it on him where he leant against a barbed wire fence drinking. I never saw him closer than a range of a quarter of a mile, but down the telescope he looked shortish and clean shaven and anxious – as who wouldn't be, engaged to Jeannie. Then she rushed out on to the balcony and waved to him in the best manner of the TV commercial wives thirty years later – tiptoe, with right arm up vertically and stiff fingers opening and shutting, the sun gleaming on her blonde curls, a dentifrice grin fixed on her face.

After one of these forays I realised she was still standing there looking thoughtful. 'Stephanie,' she said, 'the two most smashing men I've ever seen have just gone out of sight round the cliff.'

'Oh yes,' I said, tipping coal savagely on the fire.

'They just might,' she said, 'have accidentally thought I was waving at them.'

Ten minutes later they came up the hill behind the Signal Station. Even I could hardly believe they were real. Nobody off a film set could possibly be so bronzed, broad-shouldered, curly-haired, clean, and as it turned out charming, courteous and polite. Their uniform was exquisite in its ranges of palest ochre and sepia. Their shoes looked like hand made leather from the Burlington Arcade. On their shoulders a leaping Springbok stood out dazzlingly. They were South African Air Force.

'Mind if we come up?' they said.

I said, 'I'm afraid I can't ask you in, I'm not allowed to, but if you'd like a cup of tea wait there and we'll bring one out.'

For once it wasn't raining. We took four chairs out from downstairs, and sat under the mast having tea, me with an eye on the sea and an ear on the telephone. They told us where they'd come from and about their homes. A couple of hours sped by. I went in to top up the teapot.

Suddenly Jeannie choked over her tea and came crashing up the ladder. She seized the telescope and swivelled it to where a little marionette figure was dancing with frustration down on the seashore.

'Do you think he could see them?' she said.

I said meanly, 'Oh yes, I should think so.'

She rushed out, said to the South Africans, 'It's my fiancé, he's terribly jealous –' and disappeared down the cliff.

They were tenderly concerned. 'We wouldn't want to upset him,' they said. 'Anyway, it's time we went back. When are you on duty again?'

I said, '1800 to 0800 tomorrow.'

At 1830 they appeared again, gallantly bearing decorative boxes of cigarettes with springboks on the lid. They enquired about Hairy. 'Och it's OK,' Jeannie said, 'he's away to the town for the evening.' We relaxed and brought the chairs and a table out again.

It was a technicolor evening, one of the Turnerish Oban sunsets. Time slipped by. We all four strolled to the edge of the cliff, the South Africans' glamorous uniforms visible for miles in the rays of the setting sun. Far below in the road a tiny figure was pacing impotently up and down. The South Africans were quite distressed by now, and asked Jeannie if they could go down and reassure Hairy that their intentions towards her were strictly honourable. She only just managed to persuade them not to, saying with a rare spark of intuition, 'You'll only make it much worse if he sees you close to.' We forgot about Hairy in the end and sat out there talking in the twilight until 0100.

As they eventually strolled off down the hill in brilliant moonlight Jeannie turned and flung her arms round my neck. 'Och Stephanie,' she said, 'sometimes I do so wish I wasn't engaged.'

We only saw the South Africans once more. They took us to coffee a few days later at Kennedy's, which was *the* place to be seen at. 'By the way,' they said, 'we went up to the Signal Station again last night to see if you were on duty.'

Our faces were stuck in horrified expressions, as we hadn't told any of the others about them. 'Oh it's quite all right,' they said. 'We just knocked on the back door and said we were lost and could they direct us to Oban. There was a little blonde girl there and she was very kind, she came all the way down the hill to the road with us.'

We sat in Kennedy's all the morning, and troops of South Africans, all unbelievably bronzed, broad-shouldered, dashing and courteous, came past and paused and asked to be introduced to us, to the chagrin of our two.

'We're going on a course tomorrow,' they said. 'We'll look you up when we come back.'

But they never returned.

At Quarters, June came up to us smirking and said, 'We had some simply marvellous South Africans up at Ganavan last night. I think they were lost. They seemed to rather like me ...'

One afternoon I was idly scanning the Firth of Lorne over a calm flat sunny sea when I saw something moving in the air behind the high bulk of Kerrera. A 'plane? Before I could wonder, it resolved itself into a vast superstructure bristling with masts and radar devices. Rapidly into sight round Kerrera, steaming north, came a battleship.

I couldn't believe I wasn't imagining it – even three miles away it was immense, dwarfing our little duckpond of sea, rearing above the mountains of Mull, hurtling along with a crisp bow wave.

There was no time for the telescope. I grabbed the Aldis and flashed out the challenge in my best morse. Instead of the code reply came slow and deliberate plain language – *Duke of York*. By the time the second K had reached me the superstructure was just vanishing behind Mull.

I got the Ops Room at Base and said as nonchalantly as I could, 'Ganavan Signal Station – *Duke of York* steaming north ma'am.'

There was a short silence. A female voice said mildly, 'Goodness me.' Then an irritable male voice came on. 'Look Wren whoever you are, if this is your idea of a joke it isn't mine.'

I said, 'But it is the *Duke of York*, sir.'

There was another pause, then an even more irritable male voice said, 'In case you didn't know, battleships don't go steaming about Western Approaches with no air or sea escort and no advance signal, and they don't come so far inshore anyway, it isn't deep enough. I imagine you saw a stray destroyer and misread the pendant number.'

I said, 'She didn't give her pendant number sir – she gave her name in plain language.'

There was a heavy sigh. 'Naval ships don't give their names in plain language. Have another look and tell me what flag she's flying.'

131

I said, 'She's out of sight sir – she only just had time to spell out *Duke of York* between the Firth of Lorne and the Sound of Mull. But I verified her outline in the identification table,' I added virtuously.

The voice sighed again. 'Wren whoever you are, if you are having me on, or have made a mistake, I'll have your kidneys for breakfast.'

'Yessir.'

Jeannie and I were left looking at the empty sea, visualising again that tremendous bulk dwarfing the heights of the Western Isles. It was the biggest ship I'd ever seen, except on Movietone News, the only battleship I'd ever seen at sea. Later, on the Clyde, I was on duty at the Signal Station when the *Warspite* came in – a thrilling sight with the crew manning ship, all the other ships letting off their hooters, and half Scotland rushing down to the banks of the Clyde to welcome her. But not so staggering as the *Duke of York* sailing past the Signal Station that afternoon in the tranquil sunshine.

'She really was big, wasn't she?' I said. Jeannie had gone quite pale. There was an expression of awe on her face.

'Och Stephanie,' she said, 'just think what a lot of sailors there'd be, on a ship that size.'

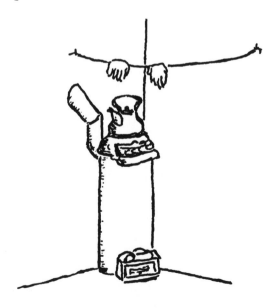

18

Coal

The summer seemed to have ended before it had really started. It was pouring with rain and the stove was belching out blackish fumes. Dave was sitting with his feet on the stove, smoking. He had brought back the mended Aldis lamp so we could stop using the spare, which didn't work properly.

'The trouble with you girls,' he said, 'is that you don't keep any booze up here.'

'Dave,' I said, thinking that he didn't really seem in a bad mood, though it was difficult to tell – at some point the iron had entered his soul, and the approach always had to be cautious. 'Dave, the Little Ganavan men have transport to work now. They pass us in the Tilly.' (The bicycles had finally rusted to bits.)

'Don't spoil it girl,' he said, 'I'm just getting my feet thawed. Why don't you put some more coal on the fire and belt up?'

'There isn't any – just a bit of slack, that's why the fire's nearly out – if it was in, your feet would be charred by now.'

'Then why the flaming hell don't you 'phone for more? Do you expect me to nursemaid you?'

'We did,' said Joan. 'Three weeks ago.'

Dave put a hand out to the 'phone.

'Before you ask Base,' she said, 'could you just mention, do you think, that I've pulled a muscle in my leg carrying the last lot of coal buckets up the cliff, and the MO says I ought not to lift heavy weights for a bit. Stephanie can't carry the lot.'

It was a long-standing bone of contention between us and Base that the sailors emptied the coal sacks to form a heap beside the road, and drove off. We had to go down with relays of buckets and carry all the coal up straight away or people pinched it.

'Give me the First Lieutenant,' said Dave, 'Morning sir, I'm out at Ganavan. The girls are right out of coal and it's very cold and wet here. I think the order is in – they ought to have it before night watch. There's no other heating. Thank you sir. And is there any chance of the ratings bringing the sacks up the hill and emptying them in the coal cellar?'

There was a quacking voice the other end. Dave rang off. 'You'll get the coal,' he said. 'As for the other, he says they've taken on a man's job, let them bleeding well get on with it.'

Joan and I trudged back to town at 1300 in the rain, and trudged out to Ganavan at 1800 in the rain. 'Are ye awa' the noo?' quavered Auld Hamish outside Raasay Lodge, with a piece of sacking over his head, sweeping gravel into little wet mounds.

At Ganavan there was a heap of coal at the foot of the cliff. The others were full of apologies – it had only just come, and they hadn't had time to get it up.

I had a battle with Joan, who said I couldn't possibly get it alone, but was obviously in pain from doing the coast walk three times in the day. I pointed out that I was so wet I couldn't really be any wetter, and young and strong, and that we couldn't get dry or warm or even have a hot drink until we'd got the coal.

I took two buckets and the shovel and skidded down the hill on the soaking grass. It was real coal, black and wet and glossy, in very big lumps. Sometimes only one lump would go in a bucket and I could only just lift it. Some of the lumps were too heavy for me to lift, and I had to bang rocks against them to break them.

Soon my hands and arms and uniform were covered with wet coal dust. I tried taking a bucket in each hand, but I couldn't keep my balance on the slippery grass in the steep part. I had to take one bucket at a time, and pull myself up on bushes with the other hand.

There was a sheep half way up. Every time I went by, it gave me an incredulous look and said, 'W-e-e-e-t.' I said crossly, 'Of course it's wet you stupid creature, if you don't like it why don't you go and live over the Border.'

It was soon dark, the sleety rain was driving in my face, and after eight buckets I was gasping and the rain on my face tasted salt and I realised it was tears. I got ten buckets up, two in the Signal Station and eight in the cellar, where they looked as big as a pound of currants on the floor, and then I went in for a rest and to help Joan light the fire which had finally given up the battle to burn on slack. I had just got my wellingtons and raincoat and sou'wester off and was holding my mauveish-black numb hands under the cold tap, when Ops 'phoned and said, 'The gale warning is over, will you take the gale cone in.'

It had been so dark I hadn't even realised the gale cone was hoisted, but it was now getting a bit lighter and I could see it sagging up the mast. 'Yes, Ma'am,' I said. I put on the wellingtons again and went out to the mast in short sleeves to wrestle with the sodden canvas weight of the gale cone, which had got its halyard wrapped round the crosstrees and wouldn't come down. I lugged it crossly up the steps to the Signal Station, noticing with satisfaction that it was now covered in coal dust, and stood it in the corner by the stove to drip. Joan had just pulled off my wellingtons, which were so wet inside they were stuck to my feet, and my soaking socks, and was rubbing my damp back with a damp sweater, when the 'phone rang. It was Ops.

'The last message about the gale cone was a mistake – the gale warning is still in force so will you hoist the cone again and keep it up till sunset.'

I couldn't get my feet back into the wellingtons so I went out in bare feet and pulled the cone up again. It would be sunset in twenty minutes, but as far as I was concerned it could stay up for the rest of the war.

It took an hour to get the stove going, and by then it was so dark I couldn't see to get any more coal. Also I couldn't stop shivering. There was an East wind, which meant the stove would belch smoke all night and we would be lucky to get a kettle to boil in another hour. We were both filthy and soaked through. We each ate a sardine sandwich, which solidified into a fishy lump just above the stomach.

I suddenly felt terribly hot, with shivers down my back. Joan put me to bed. As soon as I lay down there was a bubbling noise in my chest which kept me awake. About 0200 I got up, thinking I couldn't feel worse on my feet, and found that it had stopped raining and that Joan was sitting out on the balcony in the east wind as the Signal Station was full of smoke. The rest of the night I couldn't stop coughing.

In the morning it was pouring again. We pulled on our wet outer clothes and wet-inside wellingtons and splashed back to Raasay Lodge at 0800. The Utilicon carrying the Little Ganavan men off watch zoomed merrily past us, raising a bow wave of water which splashed us to cap level. I had a bath and went to bed, but found I couldn't sleep or even lie down as there was a full-scale orchestra going on in my chest.

By the afternoon Joan said, 'Don't you think you ought to go to Sick Bay?'

I said, 'No,' and stuck it through another sleepless night. The next morning I dragged on some clothes and walked round to Sick Bay in the rain and asked through chattering teeth for some cough medicine so that I could go on watch at 1300. The VAD took one look at me and stuck a thermometer in my mouth. Then she said, 'You'll have to come in, but you must see the MO first and he won't be here until 1800.'

So I walked back to Raasay Lodge and crawled into bed and lay there shivering and wheezing in the icy cabin all day, and then got up and got dressed and walked back to Sick Bay in the rain at 1800. By that time I didn't even care about not going on watch. It was a curious feature of Service life that Sick Bay was never in Quarters, and one always had to get dressed and undressed and walk there and back several times before admission was granted.

The MO sounded my chest and muttered something to the VAD about pneumonia.

He said, 'How many hours a week are you working?' I said, '86 hours this week.'

He said, 'How long since you had any leave?' I said, 'Six months, and then we're only getting 8 days – in other Bases they're getting 21 days.'

'That's the First Lieutenant, I'm afraid,' he said.

Then for the first time for ages I was in a warm bed, in a warm bedroom. 'We'll soon have you right,' said the VAD. 'Camphorated oil and thermogene.' And that was the only treatment I had, and rapidly I got better.

The VAD had lots of time to rub my chest with camphorated oil and stick wads of thermogene on it because she only had one other patient, a Wren I didn't know who sat silently on an air cushion with an anguished expression. I hissed at the VAD, what was the matter with her? and she hissed back that the Wren had just come back from her honeymoon. This gave me much food for thought.

The others came to see me and said they were fine and didn't mind a bit being on 2½ watches, in fact it was easier to live at Ganavan and not come back to town at all now they had some coal. They said there was an awful row going on in Base. I blenched and said, 'Because I only brought up ten buckets of coal?' 'Oh no,' they said, 'because you were quite ill, they're really worried.'

When I was better, the MO said, 'You can go back to Quarters, but don't go on duty until you get the OK from Base – I'll be in touch with them.'

I loafed around for a week, enjoying being able to have a hot lunch each day. Then suddenly a rocket of awe-inspiring pyrotechnicality rose in the air. Why hadn't I been back on duty? I was to be reported to the First Lieutenant.

Still feeling a bit chesty and blurred, I was ushered into the office of a little stout man with a red face. His office was roasting hot. In front of a roaring coal fire stood a high nursery fender. It seemed too much of a coincidence that all the rooms of senior officers had nursery fenders, they couldn't all have been nurseries before the war, so perhaps the fenders were standard equipment. I came back from a flight of fancy in which ships too were being issued with nursery fenders in mistake for ships' fenders, to find he was shouting at me. It was useless for me to explain what had happened. He roared that if I was a man I could have been shot for desertion of duty in wartime. I got fourteen days' CB.

As usual, having CB didn't make much difference in Oban, where there was no vestige of social life anyway. Fortunately we were in the midst of a drive to Cheer up the Wren with visiting lecturers. The first taught us to punch holes in pieces of leather and make writing cases, which was as good a way as any of passing a pre-geriatric existence.

The next was a strange elderly woman in a kilt and green woollen stockings who talked about 'Travel'. Captain Stokes, Naval Officer in Charge of the Base, had been inveigled into attending this lecture, to show the Wrens that the Naval Officers were interested in culture. He was elderly, benign, and venerable. Our only other contact with him was on Christmas Eve when we were taken in a truck two miles through his rhododendron drive to his front door and allowed to stand on the gravel in the rain and sing carols. He used to come down the steps slowly afterwards looking as though he was going to say, 'God bless you my dears.'

His beautiful white head in the front row lent dignity to the lecture on Travel. At question time the green-legged woman discovered that they had both been in Gallipoli in the First World War. She suddenly exclaimed, 'And didn't you think it just too too funny for words to see everybody bathing with nothing on?'

The Captain laughed rather too heartily and said, 'Ho ho, yes, of course.' The back of his scrubbed neck was pink.

She then looked intently at him and said, 'And of course, *the chess.*'

He immediately countered with a diversionary question.

We were vastly intrigued at this hint of strip chess at Gallipoli, and my fourteen days' CB sped by without my noticing.

On the last evening, when I was sitting punching holes in a piece of leather in the Common Room, they called me to the 'phone in the Little Mess. It was Dave.

'Their Lords of the Admiralty,' he said, in his sardonic voice, 'in their charity, have seen fit to promulgate a chitty to me stating that in future *if* it is raining the Ganavan Wrens may request transport from Base to go on and off duty. This privilege is not to be abused and may be withdrawn without notice.'

'Yes, Dave,' I said, feeling dizzy. 'Starting now?'

'Starting at 0800 tomorrow.'

19

Transport

'For God's sake,' said Bert from Little Ganavan one morning, 'don't tangle with the First Lieutenant again. They say he was a stoker in the First War. He hates Wrens – thinks they're stuck-up.'

'Don't worry,' I said, 'I've no intention of it.'

I was on duty with Joan, and it was raining. 'I wonder if it will still be raining at lunch time,' she said. 'I don't think it will *ever* stop now.'

It came on harder and harder. At 1245 I said to Joan, 'Do you think it's safe to ask for transport? We've got to give them time to pick up the others at 1300 and get here.' She said, 'It's absolutely black at the back – it couldn't stop by then.'

I picked up the 'phone and asked for the First Lieutenant's secretary. She put me straight on to him. 'Please sir,' I said, 'it's raining, could we have transport when we change duty at 1300?'

'It's not raining here,' snapped the First Lieutenant.

'Well, it is here,' I said.

There was a pause. Then the voice roared, 'WHAT?'

'I said, it is here.'

'It is here WHAT?'

There was another pause. 'Sir,' I said.

'If you haven't yet learnt to call an officer 'sir' you can attend my defaulters' parade tomorrow morning at 0900 for gross insubordination. And there will be no transport at 1300.'

'Yes, sir,' I said.

Five minutes later the 'phone rang. A calm female voice. 'This is 2/O Grainger from Base. I understand you are on Defaulters' Parade tomorrow morning. Would you come and see me at 0830.'

I had never come across 2/O Grainger before. She seemed interested in what went on at Ganavan and was, I think, impressed that I had come straight off night watch and walked two miles to her office in the rain without breakfast.

All I could remember about Defaulters' Parade was the same

red face backed up by a glowing coal fire, the same shouting mouth, and inevitably the same fourteen days' CB.

2/O Grainger was waiting for me after, and took me back to her office. 'I'm afraid I can't do anything about the CB,' she said, 'but there may be something else I can do, so don't give up hope. Now, is there anything you would like to talk to me about?'

Seizing the opportunity, I said, 'Yes please, ma'am, can I put in for an overseas draft?' It seemed the only way of getting out of Oban before it killed me.

She promised to put my name forward.

By now I had become quite famous in the Base and wore a kind of martyr's crown. Someone gave me her chocolate ration. My CB coincided with the whole of Quarters being gated for an offence, fairly common among Service women, involving sanitary towels, so I had plenty of company.

After I had done a week's CB, Carol and Rosemary came back from duty one afternoon in a state of high excitement. 'We've had a visit from a Medical Officer,' they said.

'Oh, him,' I said.

'No, this is a very high-up one – he asked a lot of questions about what we did, and the coal and the batteries and walking on duty late at night, and looked at the cabin and said it was scandalous. He noticed that blanket that has a sort of green mould growing on it. There was some sort of sanitary inspector there too – he looked in the lav and said it was a wonder we were not all dead from diphtheria.'

This time it was Blondie, not Dave, who brought the good news.

'You'll be glad to hear,' she said, 'that as there's a spare Tilly and driver at present you are to have transport on and off watch always. And the ratings who deliver the coal have been instructed to take it up to your cellar.'

We were so excited we decided we would celebrate by getting Late Keys and going to see Bette Davis in *Now Voyager* at the bughouse. Then we remembered that I was on CB.

'I know,' said Joan, 'We'll smuggle you out.' It was childish, but then we had been treated childishly.

We made up a dummy and put it in my bed. This was to fool the Leading Wren who did Lights Out at 2300. Lights Out was very perfunctory – she just put her head round the door, otherwise she might have had to report the state of the cabin.

I was muffled up in a balaclava and greatcoat and hustled down the stairs while one of the others diverted Chiefie to a leaking tap in the bathroom. It was black as ink outside but we knew Oban blindfolded by then. We all had a lovely cry through *Now Voyager*, and when the lights went up in the interval I buried my face in my handkerchief and sobbed. They smuggled me successfully back to the cabin. The Leading Wren had done her round and cast a cursory glance over the hump in my bed. We felt that in a minor way we had got our own back against Authority.

From then on we had the luxury of squatting in the back of a truck under a dripping awning to go on and off watch.

But I still had to carry coal once more.

I was on duty with Jeannie, who was by now married and pregnant and awaiting her discharge. We had been 'phoning the Base for more coal for the last three weeks. As soon as Carol and Rosemary had gone down the hill, I realised I had forgotten to ask them if they had made another request that morning. I thought it wouldn't do any harm anyway if Base got a second reminder, so I 'phoned and said would they deliver it that afternoon without fail as there was none left. I then went down to sweep out the empty cellar, all ready.

When I opened the door, to my horror my eyes were greeted by a mountain of coal, pressed down and running over. It must have been delivered that morning, and the others had forgotten to mention it.

I let out a yell at the shock, and Jeannie came running down the outside steps holding her stomach steady. 'There's only one thing to do,' she said grimly, 'We've got to hide the coal.'

I said, 'Where, for heaven's sake?' looking round the bare windswept cliff top.

'In the Signal Station,' said Jeannie, 'In the living room – nobody will see it there.'

'You can't carry coal.'

'No, I suppose I can't,' she said doubtfully. 'But if you fill buckets and carry them into the living room, I'll take the coal out piece by piece and stack it up on the floor.'

And that's what we did. At least it was level going from the cellar into the Signal Station living room. We covered the table with coal, and then piled it up on the chairs and all over the floor It began to look like a coal mine. When we had finished we looked at each other. We were gasping for breath and had coal up our arms to the elbow and our faces were black as night. There was a trail of coal dust with footprints in it marking our passage. I hastily swept it into the grass. With one eye on the road we splashed our faces and hands under the tap.

We had just got back to the signal room when four ratings appeared at the back door with the first sacks of coal. They dumped it in the cellar and then banged on the back door again and said, how about us coming in for a wash and a cuppa?

'No, no,' we said in girlish embarrassment, 'it's against the rules, we are not allowed to have ratings in here, we'd get in awful trouble.'

They must have thought we were very new or half-witted, but they went off muttering. We had to live with the sitting room coal for weeks until it was used up.

20

Getting on Watch

We had won the battle of transport-to-work in all weathers. Even so, getting ourselves on watch never failed to be a major undertaking. Up at 0645, breakfast at 0715, with the Duty Cook grumbling at having to get up early to feed us, then we had to collect the gear and cross the road to wait for the transport. I leant over the railing looking at the cold, grey sea curling round the cold, grey pebbles in the dawn light, and thought how incredible it was to live at the sea, to have it outside the bedroom window, and vowed that I would never, never return to the suburban commuter life again; a vow which was broken within a month of my demobilisation.

The Tilly driver tooted impatiently. It was Lady Fiona MacSavage, in a hurry to get back to ferrying Naval Officers about. The Wrens who drove the Utilicons were all out of the *Tatler*. They had long blonde hair well over their collars, and supercilious noses, and were never seen with their heads inside the bonnets of their vehicles. They never wore bellbottoms, and their long black silk legs were displayed to advantage as their skirts rucked up on the driving seat. What a contrast with the WAAF drivers, who were trousered, grubby, cheerful and practical, with their battledresses stuffed with bosom; they were usually employed to ferry pieces of filthy machinery or broken bits of seaplane about.

We hoisted ourselves over the tailboard and crouched on the floor. At Ganavan, Lady Fiona brought the Tilly up with a crisp crunch on the gravel just beyond the gap in the barbed wire. 'I'll give you ten minutes to take over and get the other two down here,' she said, crossing her legs and lighting a cigarette. 'Then I've got to get back to Base and pick up Lieutenant Commander Fiddich.'

She knew we couldn't do it – it was a hard ten minutes climb to get up the cliff, and then Carol and Rosemary had to hand over and get down, and nobody had ever known them to be ready on time.

When we'd thrown the gear out I said to Marian, 'I'll go on up with the lighter stuff and you follow – we can come back later for anything else.' I seized my pre-war holdall, which was bursting at the seams and spilling out a writing case, two pairs of stockings to darn, half a pink jumper to unravel, a pot of jam, two cheese dreams stolen from the Mess last night, an egg, and a jersey soaked in cocoa to wash. In the other hand I grabbed a paper bag of maggoty apples which someone's mother had sent, and another with two slices of cake, a frayed pair of plimsolls, a shampoo and a rusty tin of hairpins, and half a bottle of milk. As I came panting up through the heather I could see Carol on the balcony. I yelled at her, 'You've got two minutes – she won't wait!'

Carol didn't seem to hear. She had the telescope to her eye, pointing inland. I thought she must have gone mad. As I crashed up the ladder she lowered the telescope dramatically, extended her arm in a grandiose gesture, and whispered in an awed voice, 'Look ...'

I stopped and dropped the bags and suddenly it was so quiet. I realised that the sun was just coming up and the sea was a delicate pink all over, without a ripple. The mountains were deep purple near the sea, lightening towards their tops, finishing with a little fluffy cloud sitting like whipped cream on top of each. The odd rainbow was dotted about. The sky was a deepish blue, turning gold in the east, with a scattering of stars which had been left behind. The hills were covered with bracken which was stiff and frosty.

Carol was still gazing inland. 'Look,' she said again, 'there's snow on Ben Cruachan.' I looked, and the tip of the highest mountain to the east was a delicate pink, like strawberry ice cream.

Over Carol's shoulder I could see inside the signal room a large heap of ashes at the bottom of the stove. 'Oh Carol,' I said, 'you've let the fire out. And you've forgotten to hoist the Ensign. And where on earth is Rosemary?'

'Oh, have I?' said Carol. 'Never mind, it'll warm you up to get the coal. I don't know where Rosemary is – I'm not sure if she's awake yet.'

I flung myself down the ladder and into the frowsty cabin and started beating on the hump in the bottom bunk. 'Rosemary,' wake up, the transport's waiting, they'll go without you,' I bellowed. The top end of the hump moved slightly and a muffled voice murmured sleepily, 'Hi, toots.'

I gave up and started leaping down the cliff again, bathed in the pink glow of ice-cream snow, to look for Marian. She was about half way up, her hat had fallen off, she was purple in the face, with an Aldis battery in each hand. The batteries were like a primitive version of a car battery, only much heavier and more unwieldy. They had wooden cases painted black, and leather straps to carry them by, invariably broken and inadequately tied together with string, which cut a groove in your hand. Acid slopped out over their tops.

'You'll kill yourself, carrying them both,' I screamed at her. 'Fiona never said she'd got batteries.'

Marian was too puffed to reply for several minutes. 'She said ... take your something batteries ... I'm not touching them in this clean shirt ... after you'd gone on ahead ... I hid the rest of the gear behind a rock ...'

I pelted down to the road. Behind a rock a cow had one foot on Marian's hat. 'Moo,' I said belligerently and it moved. There was no sign of the Tilly. I collected from behind the rock, in three paper bags, Marian's suspender belt with a needle and cotton hanging from it, a bundle of letters, a photo album, a broken fountain pen, a hairbrush, a pre-war copy of *Home Chat* folded open at a knitting pattern for a lacy evening blouse, ten knitting needles, and a mouldy orange which we had found washed up on the beach. I started up the hill for the second time.

Half way up I passed Carol and Rosemary. Rosemary had a pyjama top and bellbottoms on. Carol was carrying two steaming pots of plum and apple jam. She said, 'There's a ship flashing.

145

And we used all the milk trying to make fudge. It curdled or something.' I didn't answer but muttered under my breath, 'And I hope you have to walk back to Base.' I puffed up the ladder, grabbed the Aldis, and acknowledged the patrol boat, which said grumpily, 'You've taken your time – I might have been a midget submarine. What on earth do you girls do up there?'

Marian nudged me and pointed to the coast road. An RAF transport was buzzing along back to Base. In the back were two tousled-looking figures in bellbottoms, sitting on the laps of two RAF Corporals. We could hear their screams of laughter as they swayed round a corner and landed in a heap.

21

Jack

One day early in May 1944, the anchorage suddenly started filling up rapidly with a convoy of ships. Most of them were US merchant ships, but they weren't the usual liberty ships. They looked much older and shabbier.

Then two cruisers, the *Durban* and the *Sumatra*, steamed in. Like the merchant ships, they had numbers painted on their sides. In a day or so the anchorage was fuller than we had ever seen it – the ships were stacked about three deep along the whole five-mile shore of Lismore.

It was a very impressive sight, until you looked at the ships through a telescope and realised that there was something odd about them. They were all quite badly damaged – you couldn't imagine how a whole convoy had got the same sort of damage. One of the cruisers had a hole right through her bows with daylight showing the other side. They couldn't *all* be waiting for a refit.

We were suddenly frantically busy – busier than we had ever been before. There was no let up, day or night. Two corvettes joined the gathering, eight trawlers, a US frigate, a tug.

The ships had no R/T contact, so we were their only link with the shore. I did a 72-hour week, my eye glued to the Aldis day and night, no time for a cup of tea. We gave up working watches, we just stayed at Ganavan as long as there was a signal to send or a ship calling up. We found we were signalling to tip-top professionals – none of the slipshod procedure we had had to make do with on the smaller ships, where one of the deckhands had probably learnt morse as a Boy Scout in 1920.

One morning I was getting desperate, with another ten signals to send before Carol came to relieve me in half an hour, and a US merchantman tucked behind another one who either couldn't see my lamp or didn't choose to answer. To make things worse, the ship in front started calling me up.

I ignored it for a bit and then sent him the equivalent of, 'What do you want, curse you, can't you see I'm busy?' as fast as I knew how. Almost too fast to read, came back, 'I know – can I relay your signals? – the guy back of me can't see your lamp.'

Thankfully, I loaded the backlog of signals on to the obliging signalman and made a mental note that No. 560, the *Matt W. Ransom*, was a useful relay ship.

At the end, the signalman flashed, 'When you have time, will you call me up? Name of Jack.' 'OK,' I said.

In the middle of the night there was a lull for a bit, and Jack must have seen the lamp wasn't flashing and called me up. From then on, that curious relationship, which is only possible by lamp, developed. As the light flickered back and forth across four miles of Scottish sea, spirit reached out to spirit, and a kind of rapport of shorthand grew, both of us knowing we were signalling so fast and abbreviating so much that nobody else could read our morse. At its best, this form of communication is far superior to speech, with the added advantages that it can be broken off at any suitable moment, and that imagination supplies the visual image – in this case of Jack who, he assured me, was tall, dark and handsome, and came from Ohio, and of me, who he fondly saw as cute and charming – in fact the pin-up girl of the *Matt W. Ransom*. Our homes, which we missed, our schools, which we had not long left, where we had been in the war, and at the end of the day – 'Kiss me goodnight, then – mmmmmmmm – that was lovely – another. Gee, you're terrific.'

The only question without an answer was, 'What are you all doing sitting in the convoy anchorage with holes through your ships?' I had to be content with knowing that most of the crews were volunteers, that they were not allowed ashore because they were under stringent security regulations, that no visitors were allowed out to their ships for the same reason, and that they had very little idea why they were there, but were so fed up and bored that some of them talked rather wildly of mutiny.

'What about you?' I asked Jack. 'No,' he said, 'I wouldn't join a mutiny, I've got you to look forward to.'

Jack wrote to me, so he said. When I got the letter, I was to reply with a photo (which would probably put paid to the pin-up dream). Surely it wouldn't take long for the letter to come four miles. But I waited and waited and it didn't come.

148

I wondered if I could break the rules about faceless communication and meet the features behind the morse lamp. I went to the American Red Cross and explained with astonishing naïveté that I had a deep relationship with one of the signalmen in the convoy anchorage, and was sure it would help his morale if I could just go across in a drifter and meet him. The Sergeant was avuncular but, I could tell, privately appalled that Jack and I had become people, not lamps, to each other. What official secrets might be evading the security net and leaking out onto that bit of sea? though Jack and I didn't know any. To go out to the *Matt W. Ransom* was completely and utterly out of the question, he said. Now at last here was the boat I most wanted to get on in the whole world, and I couldn't – there was no way round the rules.

When I got back on watch I told Jack I'd been to the American Red Cross, and the outcome of my visit. I asked him what he had been doing all day. 'Waiting for you to call me up,' he said, with what seemed to me unutterable pathos.

The pace in the anchorage hotted up, and the signals became more bizarre. 'Stand by to load all furniture onto drifter at 1800.' 'Stand by at 1500 to have all clocks and food stores taken ashore.' Where could they be going, with no food or furniture or even clocks?

Oilers and tankers joined the other ships. 'Stand by,' the signals said, 'to load ballast at 1400.' And, one day at the end of May, 'Stand by to load explosive.' We were on duty from 0800 until midnight. I did an 88-hour week.

On 30 May suddenly there weren't any signals. It had turned warm and we said the officers in Base were too hot to think up any more nonsensical messages.

On the 31st, as I climbed up the cliff at 0800, I saw that the anchorage was empty – every ship had sailed. The night watch told us, 'They went at dawn.'

We said, 'Where? Where's the signal?'

They said, 'There wasn't any signal. Captain Stokes was out there in his launch. I think he took sailing instructions out by hand.'

Later, people said the Captain had been almost in tears. He had said it was the greatest day of his life. We were incredulous – 'What, those old ships? But he was in the Royal Navy, in the Great War!'

Over the following days we speculated. Could they be to do with the invasion? But no – it hadn't happened yet. And anyway, they were practically wrecks. Were they going for refits or to the breakers? Not all of that lot together. Could they be some sort of decoy? But they wouldn't decoy a child of five, let alone the German navy. People said it had a kind of gallantry, that final convoy, headed by two cruisers, sailing out to the west.

On 6 June the invasion started, but it didn't seem to have anything to do with us.

I didn't know for years that on 7 June the *Matt W. Ransom* and the other merchant ships, led by two 32-year-old battleships, the *Centurion* and the *Courbet*, and our *Durban* and *Sumatra*, were being steered across the Channel to a watery grave. Our fleet of seventy ships joined the beetles, bombardons, crocs, grasshoppers, hippos, lilos, phoenixes, plutos, rhinos and whales of that unsurpassed, intricately marvellous creation called Mulberry.

Jack, on the *Matt W. Ransom*, along with the other blockships, sailed with carefully calculated ballast and a series of explosive charges fitted either side of each hold below the water line. While I sat in the June sun outside the Signal Station, on the other side of the Channel the *Matt W. Ransom* was held in position by tugs broadside to the shore, and then the charges were exploded so that she sank in four minutes and settled on the seabed. There she sat, overlapped slightly fore and aft by another blockship, to form a harbour of sheltered water so that supplies could be unloaded.

All through the warm summer days in June there were no ships to signal to. Everyone waited for news about the invasion. I waited for a letter.

On 13 July I was woken up from my sleep after night watch by Joan. 'There's a letter,' she said. 'It's got American Red Cross on the back of the envelope. It says on the front, sender Signalman J.C. Campbell.' It had taken two months to come four miles. Jack wrote, in a neat educated hand:

Dear Stephanie,
    I suppose this will come as quite a surprise to you, but I promised to write and I am one who always keeps a promise.
    By now you probably think I am a pretty fresh guy because

of some of the things I said by blinker. Maybe you didn't know it but I have been trying for quite some time to think of some excuse to strike up a conversation. I learned from the pilot that there were Wrens in the signal tower, so I says to myself says I 'If these girls are as friendly as everyone says they are, maybe they would consider cheering up the lonely heart of an American sailor.'

From the description I received of you I would say you are very nice. If you would send me your picture I will assure you that you would become the 'pin-up girl' of the *Matt W. Ransom*. I am making this letter short so it will not be too boring. I will be very pleased if I receive an answer from you. So don't let me down.

An admirer,
Jack

Breathlessly I wrote a reply, enclosed a photo, and posted it. But there was never a second letter from Jack. I knew later that some of the crippled blockships had broken up by then, in the violent summer storm at the end of June which wrecked part of Mulberry.

On 17 October I was in a paper shop in Oban and suddenly saw on the front page a photograph of some of the blockships. By then we had heard of Mulberry, and Overlord, but not of Corncob, which was the code name for the assembly, fitting out and sailing of blockships, nor of Gooseberry which was the sheltered water formed by a line of sunken ships.

I shook the paper in front of the nose of the stout Scottish lady who sold papers. 'Look,' I shouted, 'They're our ships, there's the convoy anchorage, they were *here!*' She looked at me expressionlessly.

'Don't you realise,' I shouted again, 'the invasion started from *here*, from *Oban!* It actually started from Oban!'

'Och awee,' she predictably replied.

I asked everyone I could think of in the Base what had happened to the crews of the blockships. 'Oh well,' they said, 'it was a risky job you know, it was difficult to get the crews off, once they'd blown up their ships. Some of them had to stay aboard. Anyway, they were all volunteers.'

For years after I used to imagine that doomed voyage of the

last big convoy out of Oban, all down the west coast of Scotland and England and across the Channel, and wonder how it felt, for men whose lives were bound up in pride in their ships, to have to blow them up so near to the enemy and then not be able to get away. And I will always wonder whether Jack Campbell is alive and well and living in Ohio or if he is lying at the bottom of Mulberry Harbour.

22

Getting on a Boat (Pleasure)

By the beginning of July things had gone quiet in Oban. There were no convoys, the landing craft had sailed, and there didn't seem to be any Navy around. Captain Stokes, who owned the launch *Caledonia*, took small parties for day trips to the islands and bays nearby. These trips were hung like jewels in our succession of uneventful days.

Some of us went to Tobermory on Mull, on a blissfully warm sunny day, still and with the sea like a sheet of glass. There was a galaxy of top brass, including the Captain and his wife, two Wren officers, and a US Navy Lieutenant. As Joan said, with that crowd we had to be on our best behaviour – no bellbottoms, but shirts, stockings, hair off the collar and No Funny Business. Fortunately we discovered that the crew were on our wavelength, and they plied us with buns and jam and tea all the way there and back.

I had been looking at a piece of Mull for nearly a year, day and night, but I had not realised how big it was until we went there. It took three hours to get up the Sound of Mull to Tobermory.

There were some Wren signallers at Tobermory but they seemed shy, fey creatures, not used to meeting anybody, and without the hard cutting edge one needed to survive in Oban. It was a tiny port, totally unsophisticated, whose inhabitants were of the smiling rosy-cheeked, bobbing-a-curtsy type, welcoming you into their little shops, instead of scowling at you as the Oban shopkeepers did.

Dorothy, Marian, Joan and I lost the others and wandered down a path to a stream where we sat with our feet in the water eating our packed lunch. There was no sound except the stream chattering over rocks and round our feet. There were no cars or people; – nothing but miles and miles of uninhabited Mull, and it was an enchanted day. On the way back we found we had been sitting on the wrong side of a fence marked 'Dangerous – forbidden'.

We met a Wren who worked in Tobermory and she blushed and wrung her hands and said they all loved it there and nobody ever wanted to leave. It seemed incredibly beautiful, but we wondered if life there might be a little too saccharine. On the trip back we lay on deck in the sun as the *Caledonia* puttered lazily along for three hours back to Oban.

After this brief glimpse of the smiling face of Scotland, we felt unsettled. The weather stayed hot and sunny, and for the first time life felt like a pre-war childhood summer holiday. We agreed that it would be perfect if we weren't so worried about rockets falling on the homes of our families in London, and what was happening in France.

Next morning when we came off watch at 0800 the sky was blue and the sun was hot and we suddenly realised we weren't tired and it would be criminal to waste the day in bed. We rounded up Marian and decided to go to Loch Awe, which was out of bounds. We did as Joan said: 'Just don't think about it – put on civvy clothes and walk to the station and get on a train – it's as easy as that and I'm sure nobody will spot us.'

We took a bottle of lemonade and some biscuits and caught the 1205 from Oban – the only train – the leave train. It felt like going on leave as we ground and chugged out of Oban, over the golf course, and stopped at Connel Ferry, and Taynuilt. Even the Pass of Brander, which always terrified me with the train clinging to the edge of the shore at the foot of a sheer grey mountain, seemed less awe-inspiring on such a lovely day.

The train was empty, Scotland was empty, we got out at Loch Awe at 1255 where there was nothing but the Hotel, and that had no guests. A man was sitting on the shore holding the painters of seven dinghies. He said, 'Would you like one for the afternoon? They belong to the Hotel but there's nobody there now. Two and sixpence for as long as you like.'

Did he sit there all the war? I wondered dreamily, as we rowed slowly out into the Loch.

In the distance we could see a very small island with a ruined castle on it. We had heard about Kilchurn Castle, which was built in 1460, and the aged crone who lived there alone, but we had only half believed it. On such a day as this, anything was possible.

We pulled our boat up, wading knee-deep through thick rushes, and tied the painter to a tree. As we approached the ruins of the Castle, a gaunt bent figure came out, with long wispy white hair and only one tooth. A small fierce cairn terrier yapped at her heels.

She beckoned us in, and then unbarred a creaking wooden door and led us into a vast black dungeon, dank and dripping. She opened a door in one corner, from which a circular staircase led up. She signed to us to go up it, while she stayed behind below. On the floor beside her were a scythe and a spade. We hesitated, wondering if she would bolt the door behind us and scream with maniac laughter and we would be walled up for ever. But we had become part of the magic, and up we went, the staircase twisting round and round up one of the towers, until we came out in the light at the top and could look round the whole width of Loch Awe with not one sign of civilisation to be seen.

When we came groping down again, she was beaming at us from a corner. We thanked her profusely and scurried back to the dinghy.

We made for another little island, about a quarter of a mile long and half as wide. It was swampy at one end, with a wooded hill in the middle, and shelving beaches with flat rocks at the other. As we came past a secluded little beach I splashed ashore with the painter. It was so hot, and the water so warm, and somehow after a minute or two we had all stepped out of our clothes and were swimming out into the Loch. Afterwards we sunbathed on our own uninhabited island.

Through the afternoon we pottered on from island to island in bras and pants, landing and exploring, bathing, rowing, or just drifting. At 1830 we began to get hungry so we got dressed, brought the boat back to the jetty, and went up to have a look at the Hotel, a huge gothic turreted building. Inside were corridors of turkey carpeting receding into infinity, mirrors, potted palms, wide shallow staircases. An aged waiter carrying a salver creaked towards us. Yes, he said, we could have dinner.

A few American officers appeared in the dining room. The waiter brought us soup, fresh salmon with beetroot, peas and potatoes, and apricots and blancmange. It cost 5/-, which seemed an awful lot to me – a quarter of what I earned a week. But Marian said you must remember it is a very big grand hotel and must cost a lot to run and it seems almost empty and I expect food does cost a lot to buy now.

We got a train back at 2030. Nobody found out that we had been out of bounds. I said, 'I think it's the best day I ever spent in Scotland.'

Lieutenant Commander Norman took fourteen of us for one more trip before the weather broke, north to Castle Stalker at Port Appin, on his small launch called *Scaup*. We perched all over the deck while he sat placidly in the stern sucking a pipe and reading the paper. It was a day of bright sun, whipping foam, tufted grass. Unfortunately it was also a day of passionate pursuit by an elderly Warrant Officer, Mr Ogilvie, of Carol. He had been trying to get her to have dinner with him for weeks. On the *Scaup* it was difficult for her to get away from his squeezing hands.

The ruins of Castle Stalker rose from a rock and were extremely picturesque. When we landed nearby on a small island, three of us cordoned Carol off and whisked her away into the undergrowth, with Mr Ogilvie floundering through a bog. We wandered on giggling hysterically, picking nuts and blackberries, with Mr Ogilvie's head bobbing up triumphantly at intervals from the middle of a blackberry bush.

Lieutenant Commander Norman stayed on board reading the paper.

We had a picnic lunch on the beach, and then some of them marked out a rounders pitch. With a cricket bat and a tennis ball, and with the three Yanks from the US Navy Office playing baseball, and us playing rounders, the game had a surreal aspect. Four of us got bored and set off across the island and found a bay the other side where we paddled. The rock pools were quite warm but marred by bright mauve jellyfish. I discovered two seagulls' eggs in a nest in the rocks, and packed them in my lunch box.

Suddenly we found it was 1715 and the *Scaup* was due to leave at 1730, when the tide turned. 'Hurry,' we shouted to Marian, sliding over rocks. But her knicker elastic had broken and she was trying to re-thread it with a tiepin. By the time we came back we were carrying our shoes and had seaweed stuck to our legs, and grass and mud all down our backs from sliding down a bank. All the Base Wrens were sitting tidily on a rock by the boat where we had left them.

Somehow there was a sad feeling to this trip. The summer flavour had gone sour. Or perhaps I had stumbled on a rare truth – that Getting on a Boat for pleasure was just a bit tame, after the real thing.

When we got back to Oban I set off for night watch at Ganavan with a seagull's egg in each raincoat pocket. Soon, an RAF transport came along with my WAAF friend Ginger driving, and she stopped and offered me a lift. As I got in there was a double crack. I spent the time until midnight trying unsuccessfully to scrub the smell out of my raincoat. The pockets were lined with green slime and it was never the same again.

I wrote:

I have found seagulls' eggs in the soft springing turf
Of uninhabited islands, watched the mottled surf
Leaping with abandoned glee upon the patient rocks;
I have sailed by night on little, secret lochs.

23
PSS

'We haven't seen a real ship since D-Day,' I grumbled to Jeannie. 'Only fishing boats, and they just dawdle about and don't bother to answer the lamp. That *Morag Jane* ought to have been back last night and she's still out. I shall forget morse soon.' I knew I shouldn't really – it was second nature now, like swimming and cycling.

The Little Ganavan 'phone gave a wheezing ring. Jeannie answered.

'Crossing on two,' said Bert.

I grabbed the telescope. 'Can't see anything.'

'I'll give you two minutes to find a surface craft,' said Bert, 'then take cover because it's a U-boat.'

I clamped the big telescope to my eye and inched it over the choppy grey sea, sweeping back and forth over the bit under which lay the second loop. Piece of wood, seagull, wave, wait – something bobbing about – it looked like a very small dinghy. Some local lunatic Boy Scout going fishing. But it wasn't moving – I couldn't see any oars. There was something odd about the hump in the stern.

I yelled to Jeannie, "Phone Bert and tell him it's OK – it's a surface craft.' I picked up the other 'phone and told Ops the bearing of the dinghy. 'It might be abandoned or have an injured man on board.'

Five minutes later a launch shot out of harbour. I couldn't see what happened, as the dinghy was blotted out by the launch. Quite soon the launch came back towing the dinghy. It flashed, 'Request ambulance on pier for injured man.'

I thought really ours was the best job in the world.

Later that afternoon the Base Officer 'phoned. 'They're very short at the Pier Signal Station – could you do night watch there tonight? Report at 2000.' I cursed mentally – that gave me two hours to get back from Ganavan, have supper, collect my gear and get to the PSS.

The PSS was, in our eyes, a poor relation. It was a hut at the end of the South pier, snarled round with railway lines, lobster pots, nets, drums of diesel, bollards, hawsers, and crates of cargo, and overshadowed by cranes. Pier was a misnomer – it did not stick out from the harbour, it was just the dirty bit of the innards of Oban bay, where the railway finished and all the small harbour craft moored. The Wrens there signalled to craft as they entered and left harbour – they could see out as far as Dunollie light if we remembered to put it on. Dorothy, who had joined up with me, and survived *Cabbala* with me, had worked at the PSS ever since we came to Oban. Recently she had drifted quietly, and probably unpunctually, off to Tobermory.

Also on the pier was the rifle range which we used sometimes, and a naval tailor who made us tiddley bellbottoms – very tight over the seat and full in the lower leg and without the three flaps fastening over the stomach. His method of measuring was perhaps unnecessarily thorough, but worth enduring for the result.

I trudged down the pier, splashing through pools of diesel and bits of gutted fish. The PSS was just a narrow oblong hut with a camp bed along the back and the usual signalling gear on a counter in front. There was just room for two stools in between. There had to be two Wrens on duty at a time, in case one was delivering signals by hand. I took over from Eileen, who had been on watch all day and did not know who was joining me.

Nothing happened except that a man from a trawler gave me a fish. I didn't know how to cook it, so I cut off its head and tail and put it in a cup of water on the upturned electric fire, and when it was soft it tasted quite nice. I sat and read my sister's latest letter. 'Dear S,' she said, 'Last night we had an enormous raid with lots of bombs. Our windows are broken and the landing ceiling is just ready to fall down, due to a pilotless plane that went off on the Ridge on Saturday night. A few days ago we put a snail in the aquarium named Molly, after molluscs, because she is one. She has already laid two lots of eggs. The Cricket Club is destroyed and a lot of damage to houses. We are still sleeping down the shelter. Can you tell me where you put the linseed oil because I want to oil my 'crosse stick?'

It was still light at 2100, and I was watching a seagull dragging the insides from half a cod on the edge of the pier when my eye was caught by an odd sight. As pied as a seagull, a newer than new Wren came picking her way daintily along between the puddles, fair hair curled off the collar, cap firmly set at the correct angle, not jammed on the back of her head, gleaming white shirt, skirt, sheer stockings, polished shoes. As she came nearer, I could see the nap on her jacket, which hadn't even gone threadbare on the elbows yet. She was only just out of the egg, her eyes were milky blue, and her hair pale and fluffy like feathers.

'I'm awfully sorry,' she said breathlessly, her Cheltenham accent not yet blurred by ragging, 'I know I'm terribly late, but I only arrived this afternoon and the railway seems to have lost my case.'

'Didn't you bring it?' I said, momentarily diverted by my incredulity at anybody not taking all their luggage with them.

'Daddy had it sent on,' she said, 'he didn't want me to have to carry it. He saw me off at Euston – he'll be awfully upset.' Her big blue eyes filled with tears. 'I'm Felicity,' she added.

'Where have you come from? What category are you?' I said, getting down to the fundamentals of how much help she was likely to be.

'From leave *actually*,' she said. 'Before that just HMS *Pembroke*. I'm awfully sorry,' she said again.

Just HMS *Pembroke* – Mill Hill – the main preliminary training depot. That was just my luck. 'Oh well,' I said, 'we'll have a cuppa. We're not busy. Could you go and fill the kettle at the stand-pipe at the end of the pier? Then you'd better get your head down. I'll wake you when you've had a few hours, then you just have to watch and, if a light flashes, wake me. I'll hear the 'phone.'

'Do I have to stay here all night?' she said, 'because I haven't brought a nightie or a sponge bag or anything. They didn't say. And it's all in my luggage.' There were bright pink spots on her pink cheeks.

I said, 'You don't need anything– just lie on the bed as you are. There's nowhere to wash.'

'Oh!' she said, 'but what about ...'

'I'll show you,' I said. It was difficult using a bucket because anyone could look in through the windows, but there was provision of a sort on the pier. I wondered what she'd think of it.

After a bit she lay down on the bed in her beautiful new uniform and shut her eyes. I didn't think she was asleep.

160

I brooded at the counter, feeling aged and cynical.

At about 0100 a shaggy male head loomed up outside the window. In an immediate reflex action my hand shot out to lock the door. It was a bony head of off-red hair, topping a lugubrious face, deeply furrowed.

'Did ye ken aboot the trawler?' it said, on a wave of whisky breath.

I said, 'No,' coldly, not wanting to get involved.

'Terrible terrible business,' it said, with r's going like a roller-coaster. 'The *Morag Jane* – they machine-gunned the survivors, ye ken.'

The new Wren's eyes were open. She came up on one elbow. Her face had gone very white.

Something clicked in my mind with the events of the afternoon. 'Are you off the *Morag Jane?*' I said.

'Nay lass,' he said. 'I was on the launch that brought the lad ashore from the dinghy. But they were all my mates.'

'Is he all right?' I asked.

'Mebbe, mebbe not,' said the man. 'He babbled a lot. They were tekkin' in the nets, ye ken, not far out from Mull, and the Sub came up almost alongside. It sank the *Morag Jane* – she went down in minutes. There was one boat – they machine-gunned that. Just the lad left alive.'

The new girl came and stood by the window. 'But how *awful,*' she said, in her high, clear voice, 'they were just fishermen.'

'It's war, leddy.' (I noticed he hadn't called *me* leddy.) 'Bluidy Germans.' He spat. The audience was making him expansive. His accent became more turgid. He warmed to his subject.

'He couldna' stop babbling about yon. It was the bluid, ye ken. It was all over everything. Splashed all up the sails. Bluid – the lads were all soaked in it. He couldna' believe there would be so much from those few fisherfolk. Slippery on the deck it was – all bluid.' His voice had become droning, monotonous. If I had been more experienced I would have realised that he was in a state of shock.

Suddenly the new Wren keeled over and with an ear-splitting crash fell to the floor, scattering tea cups, signal pads and wellington boots, and lay there motionless with eyes closed and face waxen. With another immediate reflex I unlocked the door and pulled the man in. He seized a can of water and threw it over her face, and then started mopping it with pieces of signal pad. After a minute or two she groaned but still didn't open her eyes.

There wasn't enough space for her to lie on the floor, her legs were wound round a stool and her head on the broken teapot, and we couldn't kneel on the remaining floor space, there wasn't room so we heaved her on to the bed. As we pulled our arms from under her and straightened up, I was appalled to discover that there was blood all down the sleeves of the man's shirt and the front of mine. She seemed to be bleeding fairly copiously from a gash on the back of her head. Her beautiful fair curls were sodden with water and blood. Daddy wouldn't have known her.

I grabbed the 'phone and asked Base to send help immediately. While we waited I saw the blood soaking into the grubby blanket on the camp bed and wondered how it could go on being so very red. The man talked in an increasingly high-pitched voice, his accent growing ever thicker, until I couldn't understand a word he said. I tried not to look at the blood on our shirts.

Footsteps came splashing down the pier. The pier sentry, a nurse, and poor Eileen again, blear-eyed in pyjamas and a raincoat. Between them they carried the new Wren down the pier to Quarters. Eileen came back and I put her to bed in the stained blankets.

It was 0230. I sat and thought about the men on the *Morag Jane*.

I met the new Wren in town a week later. She was wearing bellbottoms and had her hat on the back of her head. She proudly took it off and showed me a bald square where they had shaved her hair, a line of stitches going across it.

'I was a gash hand that night,' she said. 'Super Base, isn't it?' She went off with a slight swagger. There was a sailor waiting for her on the corner.

162

24

Greenock

I was packing. I quite often packed. I suffered from what would now be called a deep-seated sense of insecurity, born of the certain knowledge that I could not possibly get even half my possessions into my one suitcase, nor could I have carried the weight if I had had a bigger one. You were lucky to get a day's notice of moving, so every time the grape-vine whispered 'You're going to Lismore next week,' or 'there's a draft to Aultbea,' or Scapa Flow (it was always somewhere further north) I started, in the depths of gloom, doing up parcels of surplus possessions to send home.

I had just made a forlorn pile on my bed of a bathing costume, a book called *The Vic-Wells Story*, a balaclava helmet, a pink cardigan with holes under the arms, and an almost bristle-less hair brush, when Joan burst in.

'This time, carry on,' she said. 'We're going to Gourock tomorrow. Chop chop, we've got to get our travel warrants in the next half hour.'

'Is it north?' I said.

'No, you clot, it's Greenock, near Glasgow, south. And it's only for a month – an exchange to give us some up-to-date signalling practice and give two of them a rest.' It was July, and things had been very dead with us since D-Day.

When we collected our travel warrants, they issued us with brand new shoulder bags. These were a really imaginative gesture on the part of whoever was responsible for kitting us up. They were navy blue canvas piped in blue leather, with a zip and a carrying strap. It was the first time we had ever had anywhere to keep our hankies.

The Quarters at Greenock was Mariners, which had once been a home for retired seamen. We ate there and lived in Mariners Annexe, which was a collection of nissen huts behind. The ablution block was quite remarkable. Pairs of hot and cold taps were set round three sides of an oblong room above a concrete shelf. At the back of the shelf a shallow groove sloped down slightly along each side to a hole at the centre of the middle shelf. There was a brown enamel basin under each set of taps. When you had washed or cleaned your teeth you hurled the dirty water towards the groove and it ran along to the middle and down the hole all over everyone's feet towards a blocked-up grating in the floor.

There was a stove in the middle of each cabin, and four double bunks each side of the stove. The stove divided us into two groups of eight.

The other six Wrens on our side were coders who had all been at *Cabbala*. 'Oh my deah,' they said, 'look, they've got snow on their boots. How too too frightfully amusing.'

Two could play at this game. 'What heaven,' Joan drawled haven't we always said it would be such fun actually to *live* in the Gorbals?'

After that we shared our chocolate rations and were all great friends. They were all 18, and all from the south. Three of them had been at a Catholic boarding school together, and knelt beside their beds to say their rosaries at night. One night Clare went on so long the rest of us turned the lights out and got into bed. Eventually we heard her give a deep sigh, get to her feet and then she said loudly, in her most refined accent, 'Hells bells, I can't see a bloody thing.' The impact was colossal, as we didn't swear much normally, life was too real. There was a stunned silence and then uproar.

It was intellectually stimulating, living with sophisticated people. They read biographies and histories, they had journals on mail order, they discussed chamber music concerts. They told us how to get by at Gourock. 'It's not a bad Base,' they said, 'you're treated fairly. The work is terrific, because it's real Navy. But never eat the meat in Mariners – sometimes its got green mould on it. Otherwise the food is OK, and they cater for watchkeepers.'

Next day, when Joan and I reported to Gourock Pier Signal Station at the end of the pier, I realised what they meant about the real Navy! The Signal Station was at the top of a tower, reached by a series of vertical ladders rising through trapdoors in the floors of the small square rooms. (On night watch we used a bucket on the floor below the signal room. In the morning, before it was light, one of us had to carry this noisome slopping object one-handed down several vertical ladders and empty it over the side of the pier.)

I felt dazed at the size and scale of everything. The room was so big, with glass on three sides, and seemed full of Wrens all working flat out with lamps and telescopes and signal pads and telephones. At the back stood a Chief Yeoman of Signals, looking as professional as if he was standing on the bridge of a battleship. The chaos sorted itself out into a rigid pattern, as he barked out, 'Robinson – take that signal from the QE. Smithers – call up the AQ and ask her to stand by. Bates – answer that 'phone.'

QE – AQ – I felt I must be dreaming. I looked out at the vast expanse of the Clyde running round a great dog-leg of water from Clydebank out to the Firth and the open sea. Just sitting casually in the water quite near were the *Queen Elizabeth*, the *Aquitania*, the *Queen Mary*, and a little further downstream were several flat-looking ungainly mac-ships – the merchant aircraft carriers.

When we were on duty we were very busy indeed, but the watches were regulated with precision and we never had to come early or stay late or double up. We never had the responsibility we had at Oban, but we did have a taste of the real Navy for which I was eternally grateful – I had always had faith that there was a real war going on somewhere.

I took down a very complicated signal from the *Aquitania* one day. An hour later a sailor's face bobbed up the hatchway. 'I'm the bunts off the AQ,' he said to the Chief Yeoman. 'Which of your bunts took my signal at 1100?' My stomach plummeted. First Lieutenant, I thought, CB at least. The Chief Yeoman pointed at me. The sailor grinned, and threw a small parcel over. 'Catch,' he said. 'Nylons for you,' and his head disappeared down the ladder.

Gourock in August 1944 was on the crest of the wave, victory in sight, morale high, discipline strong. When the *Warspite* sailed in on the morning of 13 August – a lovely deadly thing, shimmering in the sun – with the crew manning ship, everyone turned out and cheered.

They weren't so paranoid about us going on boats at Gourock – sometimes we went on a launch round Holy Loch to collect libertymen (i.e. sailors ashore). But as it wasn't forbidden, the spice of danger was missing. You could get officially on the ferry to Dunoon, and on a launch to Lochgoilhead, and to Glasgow.

165

I walked back from the pier to Mariners one evening after a thunderstorm. The sky was rinsed clean to a duck-egg blue over the estuary, the air tasted like lemon juice, and the sun shone splinters in my eyes. I felt liberated from duty and I took my cap off.

As I passed the entrance to the big Army camp I caught the eye of the sentry and paused. He smiled. His eyes crinkled up and his smile was a little shy and lopsided. He had brown hair and brown eyes.

He said, 'Your hair looks so beautiful in the sun.' We seemed caught in a spellbinding moment of peace.

I said, 'You're from the south.'

'Epsom,' he said.

'But of course,' I said, smiling, 'Epsom College.'

'How did you guess?'

'You sound like Epsom College. Did you know Anthony Crowther?'

'In my form,' he said. We gazed at each other in wonder.

I've never met anyone else in Scotland,' I said, 'who comes from near home.'

'Did you ever go to Epsom Market on Saturday morning? Did you have picnics on Box Hill when you were small? Did you go swimming at the Galleon Pool at Tadworth? Did you go to Chessington Zoo and see Rosie the elephant?'

Eventually – 'Will you come off duty at the same time tomorrow?'

'Yes,' I said. 'Will you be on sentry then?'

'Yes.'

I came past at the same time the next evening but he wasn't there. There was a lot of activity – trucks driving out full of soldiers. I never saw him again. I thought, after, that he was the only man I met who really spoke the same language as I did. I suppose if there was not a war one would have met people like that all the time. But there had been a war ever since the summer I left school, and I didn't know what it was like to be grown up without one.

166

25

Glasgow

'There are six hostels,' said Joan, peering at the leaflet. 'The Girl Guide Club for Service Women, the Church of Scotland Hostel, the Central YWCA Hostel, the War Emergency Hostel, the Victory Hostel, and the Catholic Women's League Hostel. We aren't Girl Guides and I'm Catholic and you're C of E – that rules out three. The Victory is only a shilling a night and it's got 80 beds – sounds a bit rough. How about the Central? It's only got 12 beds. But can we afford 2s 3d? We get bed and breakfast and bath.' We thought we could run to 2s 3d, but it had better be good at that inflated price.

We had decided to ask permission to break our journey back to Oban by having a Sleeping Out Pass for a night in Glasgow. We had to see a First Officer, who was charming and said what a good idea to have a break and she would arrange SOPs and routeing instructions. We could leave Greenock on the 1330 on Friday, and catch the 1215 from Glasgow to Oban on Saturday. We were delirious at the thought of 24 hours' freedom.

We got to Glasgow at 1500 and went straight to the King's Theatre to book 2s gallery seats for Arthur Askey in *The Love Racket*. Then to the YWCA. 'It's miles better than in Edinburgh,' I said to Joan as they sat us down to a huge spread of fried fish, rolls, toast, raspberry jam and coffee. On the way to the theatre we bought tiddley hats at a Naval stores – they had the rim properly padded so we didn't have to stuff them round with rolled newspaper. Then we looked in at the Victory Club for tea and cakes and buns.

We couldn't afford a programme at the theatre, but we went round to the Stage Door after and Arthur Askey autographed my hostel's leaflet. A sailor said, 'I shall kidnap you one of these days, Arthur, to make me laugh on the ship,' and Arthur quipped, 'Ah, but you'll have to take me away from a little Wren first!'

It was only 2010 and Glasgow was just waking up. It seemed a pity not to see what was going on, so we hung on to each other tight and wove our way through a noisy, good-humoured crowd, made up, it seemed, of every nationality, and mostly drunk.

I said, 'Central Station is supposed to be the worst place in the British Isles.' We went past, our eyes out on stalks. It was quieter there, but very sinister. There were armed police, special police, Salvation Army, naval pickets, military police, and a row of ambulances and Black Marias outside. There were more drunk men than we had ever seen in our lives, in close knots, leering and swaying, bottles in their hands. Yanks, British, Chinese, Lascars, Negroes and there were little knots of girls in giggling groups, making forays towards the men and rushing back squealing.

Suddenly there was an eruption in one group of men, a shout, the flash of a knife, a scream, and the pursued and pursuer lurched across the station. Immediately law and order closed in implacably from either side. An American military policeman paused as he swept past us, white helmet, white belt and white gaiters gleaming. 'Have you anywhere to go?' 'Yes,' we said. 'Then get there fast, it's just beginning.' We held hands and ran all the way back to the YWCA.

When we explored the next morning, we had to admit the place was value for money. The YWCA had been the headquarters of the Scottish Women's League of Health and Beauty, and was well built, beautifully decorated and spotlessly clean. The dormitory, which had been the concert hall, had polished parquet flooring and a stage one end. There was a large empty gymnasium with a sprung floor next door. The beds were soft, the water was hot, and how marvellous it was not to wash in a brown enamel basin with someone else's toothpastey spit running down the groove in front of you. It was the best place I ever stayed in. There were only four other people there, three very dour ATS and a girl who had just been discharged from the WAAF. She talked without ceasing, about everything under the sun except what we really wanted to know, which was why she was being discharged.

For breakfast we had bacon and fried bread, butter, rolls, and raspberry jam. We took our cases to the station and then walked round Marks and Spencer eating jellies and discussing whether we should catch the 1215, or go and see *The Way Ahead* and let down that nice First Officer.

The Way Ahead was marvellous, and David Niven was absolutely wizard, and we cried at the end when he walked on into the battle smoke.

When we came out it was 1500 and we were starving. We found the NAAFI where we had savoury pie, potatoes, carrots, cauliflower, gravy, then rhubarb tart and custard and Horlicks. They gave us tomato rolls and shortbread and doughnuts for the journey. The whole lot came to 1s 7½d each, and we each had a free meal order for 1s 6d.

We got the 1715 to Oban and threw our routeing instructions out of the window.

'What do you remember most?' said Joan.

I thought. Glasgow and Gourock seemed a jumble of bright colours and larger than life impressions. 'I think I remember most the *Warspite* sailing up the Clyde,' I said.

But in my heart I thought, really I remembered most the sentry who said my hair was beautiful.

It was still light in Oban at 2130, with a moon coming up over the harbour. Auld Hamish was leaning on the gatepost stuffing what looked like seaweed into his pipe. 'It's a braw brecht moonlicht nicht the nicht d'ye ken,' he said.

'Aye,' we said. We were back.

26

Running Down

Dave said, 'Welcome back from the Big City, little girl. Now you're an R/T station.'

'What does that mean?' I was getting sick of being told, 'Didn't you know? You must have been at Greenock.'

'Sorry, can't wait,' said Dave. 'Got to get my hair cut.' And he was away down the cliff, calling over his shoulder, 'Call sign "Claymore", okeydoke?', his rather sparse sandy hair flapping in the breeze.

On the way he passed Blondie panting up. We were honoured.

'Everything all right?' she said, surveying a large grey metal machine bristling with switches and knobs and light bulbs which was sitting on the counter where the Little Ganavan 'phone had stood.

'Where's the 'phone?' I said. 'Where's Little Ganavan?'

'Disbanded,' said Blondie. 'All gone on draft. They're Running Down. You've taken over the R/T.'

'What does that mean?' I asked.

'Radio Telephony – you know,' she said. I could tell she didn't know either.

'What happens, then? What do we do?'

'Just use the Procedure,' she said. 'Dave will tell you.' Procedure was a magic word in those days, like Communication became later.

'But we don't know the procedure,' I said.

'Sorry, I can't stop,' said Blondie, casting an apprehensive eye on the grey monster. 'Got to get back to Base. Important meeting.' She shot off and could be seen ten minutes later pedalling furiously back to town.

Suddenly the grey thing sprang to life with a voice saying, very fast, in a strong Scottish accent, as if calling up the clans to Glencoe, 'Hallo Claymore, hallo Claymore, this is Bagpipe, this is Bagpipe, are you receiving me, are you receiving me, over to you, over.'

Jeannie and I looked at each other in stunned terror. I put out a hand to the panel of switches and withdrew it again. Jeannie suddenly leant over my shoulder, pressed down a switch marked 'On', and said rather high-pitched, 'Hallo there, I'm Jeannie, who are you –' and broke off on a giggle.

There was a lot of static, and after a pause we heard the same voice mutter, 'Bleddy women everywhere, sir.' A clipped voice, southern accent, came on saying, 'Hallo Claymore, hallo Claymore, please use correct procedure, over to you over.'

Suddenly I saw a steely look in Jeannie's eye. She snapped down the switch again and said very fast into the receiver, 'Hallo Bagpipe, hallo Bagpipe, this is Claymore, this is Claymore, receiving you loud and clear, go ahead please, over to you over.'

There was dead silence from the machine.

'How on earth did you know?' I said.

She looked deprecating. 'Och it was in the film,' she said, 'you know, the one at the bughouse last week, about the Yanks winning that battle, Alamein I think it was, or was it Dunkirk?'

The next time I did night watch with Jeannie I got to bed at 0400 leaving her on watch. Something woke me out of a deep sleep. A sort of rhythmic insistent beat. Pom te pom te pom te pom te pom te *pom pom*. I slid silently out of my mattress cover and crept up the ladder. There she was, hopping and jigging and clicking her fingers, with her head on one side. 'Jeannie!' I yelled. 'Put it back on our wavelength at once!'

'Och Stephanie,' she said, 'don't be a spoil sport! It's Glenn Miller, it's "In the Mood"', and she chanted 'Hiya Mr Whatsit what you doin' tonight ...?'

I wavered. Glenn Miller. But stern duty called. As I switched it back an angry Scottish voice was shouting, 'Hallo Claymore, hallo Claymore, have reported to Base you are out of R/T contact ...'

A few days later when I was on duty alone, there was a buzz and the clipped voice cooed, 'Hallo, Jeannie honey, how about that date?'

I snapped the switch down and said coldly, 'Hallo Bagpipe, hallo Bagpipe, this is Claymore. Please use correct procedure. Over and out.'

But Jeannie never kept that date. She had had leave to get married a couple of months before and now she kept being sick.

When I was on night watch with her, she used to cram her mouth with left over spam sandwiches and then make a bolt out of the back door and I would hear her retching in the lav. After ten minutes she would bob up the ladder again, looking pale green, and stuff more sandwiches voraciously into her mouth.

'Don't you think you ought to go to Sick Bay?' I said.

'Och it's nothing,' she said, flushing. After an awkward silence she said, 'Mebbe I'm having a bairn.'

She'll get out of Oban, I thought. She'll get right out of the whole war and be a housewife with Hairy to look after her, and have a little house and a cradle trimmed with ribbons, and a pram with a hood for when it's wet and a high chair and a play pen.

'Hallo Claymore, hallo Claymore, this is Sporran, message for you, over to you, over,' suddenly quacked the machine.

Jeannie burst into tears. 'I *hate* you, I *hate* you,' she shouted at it. 'I can't *stand* any more, I can't *stand* it, I want to go *home*, I want my *mother*, I want my *mother*, oh ...'

I flipped the switch and said, 'This is Claymore, go ahead Sporran, over to you.'

'When we get back I'll take you to Sick Bay,' I said firmly to Jeannie.

'Hallo Claymore,' the R/T said. 'This is Sporran. Request permission for compass swinging 1500 today for Canadian river class corvette, *Matane*.'

Compass swinging was quite interesting. The ships which had been in for refit sat in front of the Signal Station about a mile out and then moved around like restless hens while we gave them compass bearings over the R/T.

'Hallo Sporran, message received, over and out. Claymore.'

'I don't want to go to Sick Bay, I want to go *home*,' sobbed Jeannie obstinately, her bottom lip stuck out.

When we got back to Quarters, Jeannie sat on her bed in the cabin looking at the floor and not speaking while we all tried to say soothing things. We didn't know much about pregnancy because it didn't come into the media much then. I could only think of Scarlett O'Hara just having time to run in from the yard before her baby popped out. But then poor Melanie had a rough time, with the sheets knotted round the bed post. We hadn't got bedposts.

When we had finished being soothing, Jeannie looked up and said quite calmly, 'Whatever you say I'm going home *now*.' And she picked up her shoulder bag and got to her feet and walked out of the cabin and down the stairs.

Joan said, 'We can't just let her go like that, I mean we'd better see her on a train. There's a train to Glasgow at 1800. She'll get home tonight.'

We went after her. None of us spoke. As the train went out she looked out of the window and waved once but she didn't smile. I could see that she wasn't one of us any more.

Joan and I came back, the enormity of what we had done slowly dawning on us.

'It's worse than deserting probably,' said Joan gloomily. 'I mean, being an accessory.'

'What would the First Lieutenant do?'

'I should think dismiss us from the Service.'

We thought of not getting a reference from the Navy and never being able to get a job, and starving, and the disgrace to our families.

'They haven't got to know that we knew,' I said.

'You mean, we just happen to notice in the morning that she's not here?' Marian said.

It sounded unconvincing, even to me.

There were only three of us going to bed that night, with two on watch and one on leave and Jeannie missing.

'Lights out,' said the Leading Wren through a crack in the door, not even bothering to check. We put the lights out. Jeannie's bed seemed fluorescent with guilt in the dark room.

After hours, Joan whispered, 'Are you asleep?'

'No!' said Marian and I simultaneously, and we all sat up.

'I think we ought to tell Chiefie that Jeannie hasn't come back.'

'What's the time?'

It felt like 0300 but it was only 2300. We crept down two flights of creaking stairs, across the Little Mess, through the darkened galley, and up the back stairs. We had never been there before. At the top was a short corridor with three doors. We tapped on the first one. 'Come in,' said Chiefie's voice.

Chiefie was in bed in pink pyjamas with a lace collar, and a green slumbernet, reading an Agatha Christie.

'Oh girls, girls, you'll be the death of me,' she sighed, when we said Jeannie was a bit late back. 'Is she coming back?'

There was an awful silence. 'I don't think so,' blurted out Marian.

Chiefie carefully put a leather marker in her book, buttoned herself into a Jaeger dressing gown, pulled on tartan slippers, picked up a ring of keys from the chest of drawers and said, 'Come along down then.'

Back to the Little Mess we followed her in a chastened procession. Chiefie unlocked her desk, took out a file of papers, ran a finger down a list, picked up the 'phone and asked for a number.

'Hallo, Mrs Martin? Yes – I don't want to worry you but I just wondered if – she has? Only just come in? Oh I'm *so* glad. No, no, tell her not to worry, everything's all right, we'll sort it out in the morning.

'Now back to bed with you,' she said briskly. 'You were quite right to tell me. Poor lass.'

Jeannie had to come back for a bit, and that was when I had to empty the cellar of coal. When she went home for good they didn't replace her because we were Running Down.

One night watch in the autumn Betty rang me from Ireland. 'Listen,' she said, 'I've got a marvellous idea. You can get an exchange and come here. It'll be such *fun*.'

'But nobody in their senses would want to come here,' I said.

'That's just the point, This girl *isn't* in her senses – she's been having an affair with a Policeman, an Irish Policeman – wow! and she'll go anywhere to get out of Larne.'

It seemed worth a try.

27
Becalmed

Now there was nothing left but landing craft and VIPs. Stranded, beached, becalmed, their bright day drawing to a close, they came to Oban bay by land and sea and sat around.

We had had Landing Craft on assault courses since the beginning of the year, and sometimes had legal – and illegal – trips on them. Their skippers were Sub-Lieutenants aged about twenty, and their living accommodation was so minute that we wondered if they were ever able to sit down. Until the end of the year flotillas of LSTs and LCIs were still around, and there were rumours of an invasion of Norway.

The VIPs came in waves and included Captain Stokes, the Superintendent of Western Approaches, and ultimately the Director of WRNS, Mrs Laughton-Matthews. The only VIP who never came to Ganavan was the First Lieutenant.

For the Director's visit, both Dave and Blondie stood over us while we applied a degree of spit and polish to the Signal Station which it never saw before or since. 'And you are to wear jackets please, not seamen's jerseys,' said Blondie; 'And bellbottoms *if* they are clean and not burnt round the thighs and not done up with safety pins,' said Dave; 'And white shirts not rough dried navy ones, and hair off your collars, and no fiddley bits,' added Blondie.

In Quarters a carpet appeared on the echoing splintered boards of the Common Room, and discreetly placed vases of flowers. At lunch time on the great day we only got cold meat, and had to sit holding our hats, as it would make the passage untidy if we hung them on hooks.

I went on duty with Joan. We slung all the things which still looked a bit untidy in the coal cellar, and then there was nothing to do but wait.

When I saw eight large braided men and women coming up the hill, I said to Joan, 'We'd better put the hatch down – none of them will be able to get through it anyway, they'll have to go round outside, and with ten of us in this little space one of them might fall down it.'

'Then it'd be Court Martial at least,' said Joan.

They were all very well-nourished officers except one who was leathery and had a skirt that dipped at the back.

By the time they had squeezed their way into the Signal Station I had a moment of panic that Joan had gone, because I couldn't see her at all. She had sunk without trace behind the Director WRNS (Rear-Admiral's stripes), the Superintendent Western Approaches (four rings), Chief Officer for Oban (four rings), the Officer in Charge of the Base (two rings), Blondie, an Administrative Third Officer, Captain Stokes, and Lieutenant Commander Reggie Abbott, who, in spite of being a Lieutenant Commander, was our friend.

When a ship called up, I had to fight my way through a haberdashery of gold and blue braid to get to the Aldis. 'Request tug to help berth, as engine faulty,' said the ship. 'Tug leaving harbour now,' I told it, having 'phoned Base, 'will escort you to railway pier.' Obediently it turned and went towards the pier. I felt apologetic that it wasn't something complicated, but they all appeared deeply impressed and told us what wonderful work we were doing.

The only jarring note was when the Director noticed that we had embroidered V/S in blue silk under the crossed flags on our sleeves. All the V/S Wrens did this, to distinguish themselves from the other (inferior in our eyes) signal categories, who wore flags but were not V/S.

'We can't have all these unauthorised additions to badges,' she said. 'I must look into it.' Immediately the other Wren Officers said 'Yes ma'am,' in chorus, and whipped out little notebooks and made notes.

I thought how sad it was that the Director couldn't see us as we really were, because the Signal Station that afternoon bore no resemblance at all to real life. I knew that she had pioneered R/T Wrens in 1917, so there couldn't be much she didn't know about signals, although as a participant in the Great War she was to me a sort of latter-day Ancient Mariner by now.

'Can I see the living quarters now?' said the Director. The procession wended its way out on to the balcony and down the

176

outside ladder and round the back, while Joan and I pulled up the hatch, hurtled down the inside ladder, and flung the back door open to welcome them, like in a French farce.

In the evening, there was a compulsory sing-song in Quarters, and a little talk by the Director about our responsibilities as Mothers of the Future and how we must take the knowledge we had gained in the Service into our own homes. Joan dug me in the ribs. I couldn't at that moment think of any knowledge the Wrens had given me which would equip me for the future, except as a coalheaver.

Afterwards they rolled up the carpet and put it away.

There then set in a period of great boredom, when we began to feel more and more as if it was the Brownies we had joined. We had a competition to see who could scream the loudest. We made a pinup gallery all round the Signal Station of sexy men from the film magazines. Marian wrote a poem:

> Eight little Gana-Wrens
> Thought transport would be heaven –
> One asked the First Lieutenant
> Then there were seven.
> Seven little Gana-Wrens,
> One got in a fix;
> Her Wren days were over –
> Then there were six.
> Six little Gana-Wrens,
> Very much alive,
> One went to fetch some coal,
> Then there were five.
> Five little Gana-Wrens
> Scrubbed the SS floor;
> One fell down the hatchway,
> Then there were four.
> Four little Gana-Wrens
> Signalled Yanks at sea;
> Strictly unofficial,
> Then there were three.
> Three little Gana-Wrens
> Feeling very blue;

One asked for a wireless,
Then there were two.
Two little Gana-Wrens
With one stand-easy bun
Fought a duel for it,
Then there was one.
One little Gana-Wren
Couldn't bear the thought
Of being on perpetual watch,
Then there was nought.

I went on an Overseas Board. The Officer said that V/S Wrens really never went abroad because of being on watch in isolated places and all those men and there might be Funny Business. She said what a pity because she had interviewed about fifty Wrens that week and I was the only one who wanted to go – the others seemed to be afraid of malaria or torpedoing or rape. Privately I thought that any of these would be preferable to Oban.

Reggie Abbot, the Lieutenant Commander who was our friend, and had settled in Oban with his wife, dropped in quite often at the Signal Station – he said it was the only place outside his own home where he could always be sure of a warm welcome and a good cup of tea. He tried to arrange duty trips on boats for us, which were vetoed by the First Lieutenant, and drafts to Lismore, which were vetoed by Chief Officer.

In Quarters, they arranged a social and invited twenty sailors from a camp nearby. The social started at 1930, and at 2100 the first six sailors rolled in, so dead drunk they couldn't get through the door and were sick on the step. They had been drinking since they were let out of camp at 1700.

I took to going for long walks alone. One afternoon I struck up inland towards the circle of mountains behind Oban. It was very grey and bleak and silent. I squelched along, up to my ankles in a bog, with sharp rushes slashing my calves. There were large black birds, possibly vultures, hovering overhead.

As I climbed higher onto the foothills, I was on treacherous rocks, ill-balanced on each other, with occasional deep rifts widening into crevasses. I reflected that if I fell down one, or even sprained my ankle, nobody would ever find me. In fact probably

178

they would not even notice my absence. I came over a high pass on to steep sloping ground and lost my footing. My feet shot from under me and I slithered down about half a mile of rough scree.

When I got to my feet I was on tarmac. In fact I was on the main road just out of Oban, and a group of pedestrians was staring at me in astonishment. I hobbled back into town along the road.

Another day I was walking through the town with Carol and Rosemary complaining bitterly. 'Over a year I've been here,' I said, 'and I don't know anybody at all.'

At that moment a naval officer approached, swept off his cap, gave a little bow, said, 'Good morning, Stephanie!' and passed by. The others would never believe that I had no recollection of ever having seen him before. I thought that he must have been a phantasm provided by the fates to placate me.

In November, one of the patrol trawlers, the *Southern Wave*, went to the breakers' yard, and the last ship left the convoy anchorage. On Christmas Day I was on duty for nineteen hours, alone for ten of them. There had only been five of us for months. There was nothing left to signal to.

On 21 February 1945 they closed the Signal Station. We pinched all the souvenirs we could detach from the actual fabric. Then, all together for the first time since October 1943, we walked into town to the Gem Box and bought silver Galley of Lorne brooches, which we had engraved on the back 'Ganavan 1943-45'.

In the evening we went on the bus to Connel Ferry and had dinner at the Falls of Lora Hotel. We each kept looking round at the other four, feeling that somebody was missing.

But it was Ganavan that was missing, the place we had loved, without knowing it, as much as one loves a person. 'It's all alone,' said Carol. 'No light at all. No 'phone. No lamps or telescopes. Empty. Nothing.' Tears came into our eyes as we bent over the tinned pears and custard.

The next day the other four went on draft, and I was transferred to the Signal Distribution Office to await my draft to Larne. For once, I had an excuse to stay packed. This time, on top of my clothes was the tattered White Ensign from Ganavan. Nobody had missed it and it comforted me. There was already a rumour that one of the Oban ladies wanted to buy the Signal Station for a summer bungalow.

I left Oban for the last time on 1 March. There was nobody left to see me off except Auld Hamish, propping up the gatepost. As I passed him I said, 'I'm awa' agen.' He scowled at me. 'Och awee and dinnae blether,' he said. I got the midday train to Stranraer, and a First Class cabin on the Irish Sea boat, with sheets, hot and cold water, and a stewardess. As it left the quay, physically I left Scotland for ever.

Mentally, I should never get away. Ganavan would haunt me. Never again would I be so bored, so busy, so cold, so wet, so hungry, so tired. Though I have hardly ever since been where I wanted to be, never after did I feel so trapped in a place with no prospect at all of escape. Later relationships with other people may have been based on much closer ties of interest and experience, but none had the same flavour of shared adversity and of passionate pride in the job and the privilege of service with the Royal Navy.

Never again would any job give me the satisfaction I had when I held the Aldis in my hand and said to a large ship, 'Turn to starboard', and it did. If only I could have been a coastguard after the war, with a little white-washed house and white-washed stones up the path, I would have sat there for the rest of my life, utterly happy. So I thought.

But there was always a nagging doubt. All that hardship and privation – was it the true reality of life, or was it a highly-coloured version of the boarding school none of us had ever been to? Did we really help to win the war, or were we just playing at sailors? After a war, only a few fortunate people live to be sure they really had the glory. For the rest of us, we wonder as we get older if it was worth it, as the penalties of war become more apparent, and one realises that, once started, a war is never over in the lifetime of the people who have fought in it. In the looking-glass world of war, the ones who die are the winners, and the losers are those who have to go on living without them.

During the snippety package-tour years, the 'fifties and 'sixties, I would be going to Austria, Spain, Malta, Greece, Italy, Norway, Portugal, France, Belgium, not to mention Wales and almost every county of England from Yorkshire south. But I never went back to Scotland, never. Perhaps I was afraid to find out it wasn't so awful as I remembered, and perhaps I was afraid to find out it was worse.

In the meantime, there was Ireland. I gave never a thought to the heartsick Irish girl, crossing in the opposite direction, bound for Oban. When I looked out of the porthole in the morning, there were low green hills on the horizon, over the calm sea.

Lament

The stolen, crowded moments fly,
 Too fragile is this breathing space;
Too soon his eager frame must lie
 Forlornly in some foreign place;
My heart cries out that he will die,
And I have never seen his face.

For these few weeks he wanders free,
 Yet dimly comprehends the choice
Which he has made, forsaking me;
 No memories my hours rejoice;
A world of silent grief I see,
For I have never heard his voice.

Bitter it is that he must die
 Before our love was young and glad;
Yet though I know that, in him, I
 Must lose the things I never had,
Harder it is to feel that he
Will never know those things in me.

Written in Ganavan Signal Station, 1944
First printed in *More Poems of the Second World War*, ed. Victor
Selwyn, pub. J. M. Dent 1989

III

Finding Jack

1

A Telephone Call

It is June 4th 2000, 8 am on a Sunday morning. The 'phone rings: a lady's voice, an American accent: 'Is that Stephanie Batstone?' I say, 'Yes'. Long pause. Voice continues, sounding very nervous. 'Did you – did you ever hear of Jack Campbell? In the war?

I can only remember shouting, 'It can't be true, it can't be true!' and 'How did you find me?'

'I was looking at a magazine', she said. 'There was something about D-Day and the blockships. It gave your name.' She kept saying, 'I must go now, they've called our flight.' And I was shouting, 'You can't go now, who *are* you? Give me an address.' And eventually she said, 'Oh, I'm his daughter, and she gabbled an address and was gone.

I spent a day in a mental whirl. Then the next day Nicki 'phoned again, from the States, and we exchanged a lot of news. Then came a letter from Jack, 56 years on, and his photo, and everything started happening.

I read the letter, and I sat and thought of all the years since Mulberry and the blockships. I remembered all the men and women friends who have shaped my life since the war, and Jack, a tiny pinpoint of light, receding over the years.

I thought of the dead-end typing job after the war, the dreary bedsitters in London, the sudden breakthrough to a professional career, my climb to the top of my tree.

And then the branch broke and I was down the bottom again, facing early retirement, with no job and not much money.

I went on a 'How to write a book' course, for something to do. I had recently been to a memorial service for Lord Louis Mountbatten, and I started to write about the war. The other students were spellbound when I read it out to them, and begged me to go on with the story.

When I got home, I discovered that my mother had kept all the letters I wrote to her during the war. (How amazed she would have been to know that they finished up in the Imperial War Museum.) Retirement became the time to write a book.

I tried over forty publishers. 'The war is all old hat now, dear,' they said, 'Nobody is interested in the war any more. We'll never be able to sell a war book again.'

Come on, Jack! We'll prove them wrong yet.

2
Jack's D-Day

Nov. 22, 2000

Dear Stephanie:

I'm very thankful for that newspaper article about you looking for me. I'm also thankful for the opportunity to write all these memories down. It seems like I was a very small spot in time, proud to be serving my country and doing whatever job I was asked to do. Our branch of the U.S. Navy was not very glamorous, but we were able to complete our mission.

I quit my job at the Curtis Wright aircraft factory and in November 1942 I enlisted in the US Navy! They sent me by train to Great Lakes Naval Training Center, just north of Chicago, Illinois. You're probably familiar with the sequence that followed: shots – marching – more shots – more marching. I got pretty good at marching but I never was very good with the shots.

At the end of boot camp, individuals were given assignments – either going to the fleet or being sent to some training school. Since I could type fairly well, they had me scheduled for storekeeper school, but our Company Commander, who I got along with very well did not think I would like that job and he asked if I had any other preference. I mentioned signal school, and he arranged for me to go to the University of Chicago, where I graduated at the top of my class and received a 3rd class petty officer rating.

After signal school a group of us were sent to Norston Heights, Connecticut for gunnery training. From there we were moved to Brooklyn, New York, and attached to the U.S. Navy Armed Guard (gun crews on merchant ships).

I went on board my first ship July 4th 1943. It was a tanker that had seen better days, but it was a thrill to be going to sea for the first time, on the *Gulfhawk*. I was on this ship seven months and made trips to Scotland, Algiers, N. Africa and Gibraltar.

Our gun crew went on board the *Matt Ransom* on February 12th 1944 in New York

One thing we noticed about her condition was a large patch just aft of the starboard bow. This was evidence that the ship had struck a mine on one of her trips at sea. It also resulted in a buckling of the main deck just forward of the wheel house. We came to the conclusion that this ship had seen better days!

We sailed from New York to Halifax N.S., which was a staging area for North Atlantic convoys. When we arrived in Halifax it was snowing very hard. Once we dropped anchor in the channel our gun crew had a great snow-ball battle. We sailed from Halifax for England in convoy.

Our first port in England was Milford Haven, where we unloaded our cargo. In Newport various parts of the ship were removed, such as winches, booms etc., and this was where they cut away the bulkheads below deck, to facilitate the sinking at Normandy. We then sailed to Oban.

It's very difficult to remember how I felt before and during the Normandy invasion. It was an awesome experience.

I guess the first feeling it was really happening came on the morning of June 6th when the bombing raids were going on. I never saw, nor will I ever see again, that many airplanes flying over at one time. All heading across the Channel. It gave you the feeling that this was big!

When our convoy reached the Normandy coast on the morning of June 7th, there were ships of every description in all directions. A pilot came on board the *Matt Ransom* and the Merchant Marine crew was evacuated from the ship.

An army tug started moving us to our location, and we became aware that the beaches were not totally secure. A battleship was firing 16-inch shells toward some beach emplacements in hope of eliminating German 88s that were still active. A destroyer passed us about 500 yards off our port side, firing all her guns toward shore.

In order to provide the break-water at Utah beach, the first of our ships ran aground, bow first. The second ship was secured bow to stern of the first ship, exploded her charges and sank rapidly. The *Matt Ransom* was third in line. Our bow line was secured to the ship ahead and our explosive charges were fired.

Things do not always work as planned! The *Ransom* began to sink stern first, and, breaking the lines, pulled away from the

190

second ship. Army tugs tried frantically to keep us in position, but lines snapped as fast as they could be put aboard. The ship finally settled on the bottom with a gap between us and the second ship that had to be filled with two of the ships behind us.

Before our ship was scuttled, someone in our crew suggested that we empty the freezer, which would eventually be under water. We brought up a good supply of frozen beef and stacked it high and dry on deck. It didn't take long to get word to some army personnel who were operating small boats in the area. These G.I.'s took all that beef back to their mess sergeant and we were thanked later for much improving their menu.

The first night in our new 'position' was mostly spent at 'general quarters', because we had received information that German torpedo boats were in the area. No torpedo boats were spotted but a low-flying aircraft was sighted coming in our direction. Well, it was dusk and visibility was not good and every ship in the harbor opened up on that plane, including us. As it passed directly over us, we could see the stripes on the wing, indicating it was an American plane. As it moved away from us, a shell exploded under the plane, bringing it down. We were later informed by loud-speaker from a launch that it crashed fifty yards from a field hospital and that the pilot parachuted to safety. We were warned to be more observant!

For the life of me I can't remember what meals we ate, sitting on Utah beach. It probably was K rations but I'm not sure. I do recall, one evening our gunner officer decided to surprise us with some chocolate pudding he prepared. It looked great but he mistakenly used salt instead of sugar: you can guess the rest.

We had a very good gun crew aboard the *Matt Ransom*: approximately eighteen guys and an Ensign gunnery officer. Thank heavens, all came through the episode unharmed.

When we were evacuated to an LST for the trip back to England, it was a very sobering experience because the ship was loaded with wounded men. There was also a captured German general and his aide on board. Whenever the general was escorted among the wounded men you could see the anger, and many of them made an effort to get up and go after this guy.

Our crew was placed below deck at the bow of this LST. We were given a stretcher to sleep on and a blanket for cover. As I was sleeping soundly, there was a hand on my shoulder and a voice asking 'How are you, son?' He was an army doctor who thought I was one of the wounded.

After returning to the States, I was assigned to a communication crew, or as we were known 'Commodore Crew', which handled communications in convoys. I was on ten different ships and sailed to ports in Trinidad, Southampton, Liverpool and twice to Oran, N. Africa. When the war was over in Europe, I was transferred to the Philippines and then to Okinawa, where we were making plans for the invasion of Japan. The atom bomb brought an end to that possibility.

I got carried away with this letter. Some things I don't think I've talked about since they happened.

Stay well, and keep that typewriter in good working order, because we're not done yet.

Best regards,

Jack

—·— · · —··— ·— ··· —— ·· ·—· ·

——— —· —·—— ——— ··— ·—·

··— ·— —·— · ·— —· —·· ·—

··· ——— — —· ·—— ·· —· —·—— ———

··— ·—· ···· · ·— ·—· —

Stephanie and Jack meet again, outside the Imperial War Museum on 6th June 2001, with the press in attendance.

Photograph by Audrey Quine